# Complete Guide to Human Resource Management

## A Step by Step Guide to Personnel Management

I0462909

### By Meir Liraz

Published by BizMove
www.bizmove.com

# Table of Contents

# 1. Basics of Human Resource Management

Personnel management is concerned with the effective use of the skills of people. They may be salespeople in a store, clerks in an office, operators in a factory, or technicians in a research laboratory. In a business, personnel management starts with the recruiting and hiring of qualified people and continues with directing and encouraging their growth as they encounter problems and tensions that arise in working toward established goals.

In addition to recruiting and hiring, some of the responsibilities of a personnel manager are:

1. To classify jobs and prepare wage and salary scales.

2. To counsel employees.

3. To deal with disciplinary problems.

4. To negotiate with labor unions and service union contracts.

5. To develop safety standards and practices.

6. To manage benefit programs, such as group insurance, health, and retirement plans.

7. To provide for periodic reviews of the performance of each individual employee, and for recognition of his or her strengths and needs for further development.

8. To assist individuals in their efforts to develop and qualify for more advanced jobs.

9. To plan and supervise training programs.

10. To keep abreast of developments in personnel management.

To understand the personnel manager's job think of how you would deal with the following examples of challenging employee situations:

The firm's employees - especially the most qualified ones - can get comparable, if not better jobs with other employers.

When a firm faces a scarcity of supervisory and specialized personnel with adequate experience and job capabilities, it has to train and develop its own people. This can be time consuming and expensive.

The cost of hiring and training employees at all levels is increasing, for instance, several thousand dollars for a salesperson. A mistake in hiring or in slow and inefficient methods of training can be costly.

Personnel managers must comply with the law by employing, training and promoting women and persons from minority groups. The problem in doing so is that many of these employees have not had appropriate experience and education in the past.

Most employees, whether or not represented by labor unions, continue to seek improvements in direct compensation, employee benefits, and working conditions. All commitments must be based upon what the firm can afford, comply with current practices of other employers, and be understood and accepted by the employee. To do this, all employee policies and operating procedures should be developed and negotiated with great care.

Some employees may not perform satisfactorily simply because their firm offers competitive compensation, benefits, and working conditions. In addition to these financial or physical compensations, they want responsibility, the opportunity to develop, and recognition of accomplishment in their jobs.

The law have established requirements for pension and other benefit plans, and also bar mandatory retirement at age 65. Complying with such changes presents real challenges.

Personnel management works to achieve practical solutions to such problems. In large firms, it generally provides support to line management. In this staff capacity, the personnel department has the responsibility to develop and implement policies, procedures, and programs for recruitment, selection, training, placement, safety, employee benefits and services, compensation, labor relations, organization planning, and employee development.

Often, the owner-manager of a firm also has to be the personnel manager. In such a case it is necessary to have an overview of current trends and practices in personnel management.

All small businesses must staff their operations. This involves bringing new people into the business and making sure they are productive additions to the enterprise.

Effective human resource management matches and develops the abilities of job candidates and employees with the needs of the firm. A responsive personnel system will assist you in this process and is a key ingredient for growth.

Human resource management is a balancing act. At one extreme, you hire only qualified people who are well suited to the firm's needs. At the other extreme, you train and develop employees to meet the firm's needs. Most expanding small businesses fall between the two extremes i.e., they hire the best people they can find and afford, and they also recognize the need to train and develop both current and new employees as the firm grows.

One function of personnel management deals with how to hire and train the right people and addresses the characteristics of an effective personnel system, such as:

Assessing personnel needs.

Recruiting personnel.

Screening personnel.

Selecting and hiring personnel.

Orienting new employees to the business.

Deciding compensation issues.

Another function addresses the training and development side of human resource management. A third function deals with how the personnel system and the training and development functions come together to build employee trust and productivity. These three functions stress the importance of a good human resource management climate and provide specific guidelines for creating such a climate.

## Human Resource Management Audit Questionnaire

Does the business have a plan for forecasting long-term personnel needs?

Are there guidelines for hiring personnel, or are employees hired based on gut feelings?

Are there job descriptions for all positions?

What do employees like about their jobs?

What do employees dislike about their jobs?

Why do employees leave the organization?

Is there an active training program? Is it based on an assessment of where the firm is now or where it should be in the future?

Are a variety of training programs available?

How is morale in the firm?

Do employees really believe what you have to say?

Are all employees treated fairly?

## 2. Developing a Personnel System

### Assessing Personnel Needs

The small business owner should base the firm's personnel policies on explicit, well-proven principles. Small businesses that follow these principles have higher performance and growth rates than those that do not follow them. The most important of these principles are

All positions should be filled with people who are both willing and able to do the job.

The more accurate and realistic the specifications of and skill requirements for each job, the more likely it is that workers will be matched to the right job and, therefore, be more competent in that job.

A written job description and definition are the keys to communicating job expectations to people. Do the best job you can! is terrible job guidance.

Employees chosen on the basis of the best person available are more effective than those chosen on the basis of friendship or expediency.

If specific job expectations are clearly spelled out, and if performance appraisals are based on these expectations, performance is higher. Also, employee training results in higher performance if it is based on measurable learning objectives.

The first step in assessing personnel needs for the small business is to conduct an audit of future personnel needs.

Ask yourself

Can the workload you visualize be accomplished by the present work force? Will more or fewer employees be needed? Consider seasonal patterns of demand and probable turnover rates.

Can any jobs be eliminated to free people for other work?

What balance of full-time or part-time, temporary or permanent, hourly or salaried personnel do you need?

What does the labor supply look like in the future?

Will you be able to fill some of the jobs you've identified? How easily?

What qualifications are needed in your personnel?

Develop a method to forecast labor demand based on your answers to these questions. Once your needs are estimated, determine strategies to meet them.

The process of selecting a competent person for each position is best accomplished through a systematic definition of the requirements for each job, including the skills, knowledge and other qualifications that employees must possess to perform each task. To guarantee that personnel needs are adequately specified, (1) conduct a job analysis, (2) develop a written job description and (3) prepare a job specification.

## Job Analysis

Job analysis is a systematic investigation that collects all information pertinent to each task performed by an employee. From this analysis, you identify the skills, knowledge and abilities required of that employee, and determine the duties, responsibilities and requirements of each job. Job analysis should provide information such as

Job title.

Department.

Supervision required.

Job description-major and implied duties and responsibilities.

Unique characteristics of the job including location and physical setting.

Types of material used.

Types of equipment used.

Qualifications.

Experience requirements.

Education requirements.

Mental and physical requirements.

Manual dexterity required.

Working conditions (inside, outside, hot, cold, dry, wet, noisy, dirty, etc.).

## Job Description

The job analysis is used to generate a job description, which defines the duties of each task, and other responsibilities of the position. The description covers the various task requirements, such as mental or physical activities; working conditions and job hazards. The approximate percentage of time the employee should spend on each activity is also specified. Job descriptions focus on the what, why, where and how of the job.

There is an excellent resource the small business owner can use to develop job descriptions, ask employees themselves to describe their jobs. A good employee may know more about the job than anyone else.

## Job Specification

The job specification describes the person expected to fill a job. It details the knowledge (both educational and experiential), qualities, skills and abilities needed to perform the job satisfactorily. The job specification provides a standard against which to measure how well an applicant matches a job opening and should be used as the basis for recruiting.

## Recruiting

As a small business owner-manager, you should be aware of the legal environment in which you operate. This is especially true when it comes to recruitment. Being aware of legislation that will affect your business is extremely important to efficient recruiting.

## Sources of Employees

Effective recruiting requires that you know where and how to obtain qualified applicants. It is difficult to generalize about the best source for each business, but a description of the major sources follows.

**Present employees** - Promotion from within tends to keep employee morale high. Whenever possible, current employees should be given first consideration for any job openings. This practice signals your support of current employees.

**Unsolicited applicants** - Small businesses receive many unsolicited applications from qualified and unqualified individuals. The former should be kept on file for future reference. Good business practice suggests that all applicants be treated courteously whether or not they are offered jobs.

**Schools** - High schools, trade schools, vocational schools, colleges and universities are sources for certain types of employees, especially if prior work experience is not a major factor in the job specification. Schools also are excellent sources for part-time employees.

**Private employment agencies** - These firms provide a service for employers and applicants by matching people to jobs in exchange for a fee. Some fees are paid by the applicants, and there is no cost to the employer; for highly qualified applicants in short supply, the employer sometimes pays the fee.

**Employee referrals** - References by current employees may provide excellent prospects for the business. Evidence suggests that current employees hesitate to recommend applicants with below average ability. Word of mouth is one of the most commonly used recruiting sources in the small business community.

**"Help Wanted" advertising** - Letting people know that the business is hiring is a key element in gaining access to the pool of potential employees. At its simplest, this type of advertising may take the form of a Help Wanted sign in the window. More sophisticated methods involve using local media, primarily print sources such as daily and weekly newspapers. The classified pages of newspapers are frequently consulted by active job seekers, including currently employed individuals who may be tempted by a more attractive position. Other advertising media include radio and television. These tend to have a wider appeal than the newspaper; however, the price of an advertisement is correspondingly higher.

Specialty media publications, such as trade association magazines and newsletters, may also produce quality job applicants. There are efforts in some parts of the country to offer small business employers access to cable television community bulletin boards. Another high-tech opportunity is to list positions on computer network bulletin boards.

Prices for help wanted advertising vary and the small business owner approaches them with caution. A well-placed, high-quality advertisement will attract good people, whereas, an expensive advertisement in the wrong medium may get no results. Some experimentation is worthwhile to most small businesses. Another suggestion is to ask other small business people in the area about their success with help wanted advertising. Learn from others' successes and mistakes.

## Screening

The screening process provides information about an individual's skills, knowledge and attitudes, enabling a potential employer to determine whether that person is suited to, and qualified for, the position. Experience has shown that hiring an overqualified person can be as harmful as hiring an under qualified person.

The application form is the place to begin screening candidates for a job. It provides information on the person's background and training and is the first means of comparing the applicant with the job description. This will ensure that you don't waste time on applicants who clearly do not meet the minimum requirements for the job.

Generally, the following information is asked on an employment application form: name, address, telephone number, social security number, kind of work desired, work experience, military service, education and references.

The personal interview is the second step in the screening process. During the interview, the manager learns more about the applicant through face-to-face contact, including observation of personal appearance. The interview should be guided, but not dominated, by the manager as it is important to let the candidate speak freely. Whenever possible, the interviewer should ask questions that are directly related to the job. Devise a list of questions that will adequately assess the applicant's qualifications while meeting the specifications for the job. Three major errors often committed in the personal interview are:

Failure to analyze the requirements of the job in sufficient detail to generate valid questions.

Failure to ask candidates the right questions to determine their strengths and weaknesses, and their fit with the job.

Too much reliance on gut reaction instead of objective evaluation of candidates based on criteria established in the job specification.

Interviewing makes the selection process more personal and gives the interviewer an overall idea of whether the applicant is appropriate for the job. The following list of techniques will help you select the right applicant for the job:

1. Review the job description before the interview.

2. Break the ice - establish a friendly atmosphere.

3. Develop an interview time plan and stick to it.

4. Keep an open mind, i.e., don't form an opinion too early.

5. Give the candidate time to tell his or her story; don't talk too much.

6. Present a truthful picture of the company and the job.

7. Listen carefully, concentrate and take notes.

8. Avoid detailed discussion of salary too early in the interview.

9. Be courteous.

10. Don't leave the candidate hanging - discuss the next step in the hiring process and the timing.

Other screening techniques include employment tests and physical examinations. Some employment tests measure aptitude, achievement, intelligence, personality and honesty. A physical examination determines if the applicant meets the health standards and physical demands of the job.

## Selecting and Hiring

If the screening process is thorough, selecting the best applicants for the job is easy. However, before making the final selection, one last step should be taken: the top candidate's references should be checked for accuracy and input. You should be aware of the tendency of references to give a rose-colored picture of applicant's character and ability. Despite this potential bias, a careful check with former employers, schools and other references can be most constructive. At a minimum, checking can determine whether or not the applicant was truthful about his or her employment history.

## Orienting New Employees to Your Business

An employee handbook communicates important information about the company to the employee. The handbook should cover topics such as company expectations, pay policies, working conditions, fringe benefits and the company philosophy toward customers.

Once an individual is hired, he or she should receive a comprehensive orientation on the general policies of the company and on the specific nature of the job. Rules should be explained in detail, job expectations agreed upon and any questions answered before the new employee begins work. New employees should be introduced to other employees and made to feel welcome.

## Compensation Issues

Compensation takes two forms: (1) direct compensation (wages and salaries) and (2) indirect compensation (fringe benefits).

**Direct Compensation -** Wages and salaries are the compensation people receive on a regular basis (monthly, biweekly or weekly). Workers are paid on the basis of time (by the hour, day, week or month) or on the basis of output (an incentive plan).

**Indirect Compensation -** Fringe benefits are an important part of the overall compensation package in most small businesses. Employee benefits now account for about 40 percent of payroll costs. The profitability of the small firm is one of the primary determinants of what benefits are offered by the firm.

One successful approach to providing benefits to employees of a small business is to allocate a certain amount of money per employee for benefits. Each employee then chooses the package of benefits that suits his or her current needs. This approach is called cafeteria planning because it is similar to going down a cafeteria line, where each customer chooses what he or she wants to eat. It has been suggested that employees perceive this approach as highly equitable because it (1) allows freedom of choice and (2) does not impose a single package of benefits on all employees.

For example, a young employee with several small children may be interested in dental insurance for his family. He is not really interested in or motivated by a pension plan at this time in his life. Another employee in this same company is in her late forties, has no dependent children and is planning for retirement. To force the same benefit on these two employees is not an effective use of benefit money. To allow some choice on the part of participants is a major advantage of the cafeteria approach to benefit planning.

Small businesses face difficult challenges when they try to match benefits with big firms. Nevertheless, the small firm can enjoy the benefits of greater flexibility and innovativeness by offering a cafeteria plan.

## 3. Hiring the Right Employees

A business is only as good as the people in it. Therefore, to effectively manage your business, you must take the time to find and hire the right employees.

This Guide discusses the process of staffing a business: setting the personnel policies, determining what skill and abilities are needed, finding applicants, developing application forms, and interviewing prospective employees.

Staffing is of critical importance to businesses of all shapes and sizes. All firms take the same risk in hiring a new employee. However, the smaller the firm, the less it is able to afford the time and costs involved in hiring and then firing, the wrong employee.

Bigger companies have developed effective hiring techniques and procedures to lessen this risk. If you, the owner-manager of a small to medium firm, are going to effectively manage your operation, you too must apply some of these staffing techniques.

### Setting Personnel Policies

First of all, know yourself. Know what business you are in. Know your own personal abilities and weaknesses, and try to anticipate how you will deal with the situations that you expect to arise in the daily operation of your business.

Then, formulate your policies in writing. Include all matters that would effect employees, such as wages, promotions, vacations, time off, grievances, fringe benefits, and even retirement policies.

Employment and training procedures must be established so that you have a better chance of getting the job done the way you want it done. You might want to consider the way you want it done. You might want to consider written policy decisions for the following areas.

## Hours

Consider here the number of hours to be worked per week, the number of days per week, evening and holiday work, and the time and method of payment for both regular and overtime work. Unnecessary payment of overtime at premium rates is a source of needless expense. By planning ahead, you may be able to organize your employee's work to keep overtime to a minimum. When peak periods do occur, you can often handle them by using part-time help paid at regular rates.

## Compensation

The bulk of your employees' earnings should come from a base salary competitive with the pay offered by other similar local firms. It may be possible to supplement the base salary with some form of incentive, such as a small commission or quota bonus plan. Try to relate the incentive to both your goals and the goals of your employees. Whatever plan you use, be sure each employee understands it completely.

## Fringe Benefits

You may consider offering your employees discounts on merchandise, free life insurance, health insurance, pension plan, and tuition payments at schools and colleges. You might also look into joining with other merchants in a group disability plan and a group workers' compensation plan. Such a plan could mean a considerable savings in your premium costs.

## Vacations

How long will vacations be? Will you specify the time of the year they may be taken? With or without pay?

## Time Off

Will you allow employees time off for personal needs, emergencies in the family, holidays, special days such as election day, Saturday or Sunday holidays?

## Training

You must make sure that each employee is given adequate training for the job. In the smaller firm, the training responsibility normally falls to the owner-manager. But, if you have supervisors, each one should recognize the importance of being a good teacher and should schedule time to teach new people.

## Retirement

What are your plans for retirement age benefits such as Social Security, pension plans, and annuity plan insurance?

## Grievances

You may expect conflicts with your employees without regard for the quality of the employment you offer. The best course of action is to plan for them and establish a procedure for handling grievances. Consider the employee's rights to demand review, and establish provisions for third party arbitration.

## Promotion

You will want to consider such promotion matters as normal increases of wages and salaries, changes of job titles, and the effect your store's growth will have on this area.

## Personnel Review

Will you periodically review your employee's performance? If so, what factors will you consider? Will you make salary adjustments, training recommendations?

## Termination

Even though this is a distasteful matter to many managers, it would be wise to have a written policy on such matters as layoffs, seniority rights, severance pay, and the conditions warranting summary discharge.

When you have developed your personnel policies, write down the policy on all matters which affect your employees and give each one a copy. Matters such as the following should be standardized and not left to the whim of a supervisor: hours of work, time recordkeeping, paid holidays, vacations, deportment and dress regulations, wage payments, system, overtime, separation procedure, severance pay, pension and retirement plan, hospitalization and medical care benefits, and grievance procedure.

## Determining Needed Skills and Abilities

The trick is getting the right person for the job is in deciding what kind of skill is needed to perform the job. Once you know what it takes to do the job, you can match the applicant's skills and experience to the job's requirements.

The first step in analyzing a job is to describe it. Suppose, as a busy owner-manager, you decide to hire someone to relieve you of some of your duties. Look at the many functions you perform and decide what your stronger and weaker areas are.

Further suppose that you have decided that you will need help in the office. The phone is always ringing. Letter which need answering are piling up. Merchandise must be ordered.

Once you have a job description on paper, decide what skills the person must have to fill the job. What is the lowest level of skill you will accept? In this example, let us assume that you decide initially to hire a secretary, but discover that secretaries are scarce and expensive. Moreover, in your area, stenographers are almost as hard to find and nearly as expensive as secretaries.

Perhaps you could get by with a typist. Hiring a typist may be both easier and cheaper than hiring a secretary or stenographer. Many high schools students are well qualified as typists, and many are seeking part-time work.

One additional point: When you start to look for someone to fill your job, make sure you spell out just what you want. Imagine that an owner-manager advertised for a "sales clerk." What should the applicant be able to do? Just tally sales receipts accurately? Keep a customer list and occasionally promote your products to these people? Run the store while you are away? The job of "sales clerk" means different things to different people. Make sure you know what skills you need and what skills you can get by with, as determined by what kind of training you can give the employee.

## Finding Applicants

When you know the kind of skills you need in your new employee, you are ready to contact sources which can help you recruit job applicants.

Each state has an unemployment service (sometimes called Public Employment, Unemployment Security Agency). All are affiliated with the United States Employment Service, and local offices are ready to help businesses with their hiring problems.

The employment service will screen applicants for you by giving aptitude tests (if any are available for the skills you need). Passing scores indicate the applicant's ability to learn the work. So, be as specific as you can about the skills you want.

Private employment agencies will also help in recruitment. However, the employee or the employer must pay a fee to the private agency for its services.

Another source of applicants is a "Help Wanted" sign in your own front window. Of course, a lot of unqualified applicants may inquire about the job, and you cannot interview an applicant and wait on a customer at the same time.

Newspaper advertisements are another source of applicants. You can reach a large group of job seekers and you can screen them at your convenience. If you list a phone number at the store, you may end up on the phone instead of dealing with a customer.

Job applicants are readily available from local schools. The local high school may have a distributive education department where the students work in your store part time while learning about selling and merchandising along with their school courses. Many part-time students stay with the store after they finish school.

You may also find job applicants by contacting friends, neighbors, customers, suppliers, present employees, local associations such as the Junior Chamber of Commerce, service clubs to which you belong, or even a nearby armed forces base where people are leaving the service. However, do not overlook the problems of such recruiting. What happens to the goodwill of these sources if they recommend a friend whom you do not hire, or if you have to fire the person they recommended?

Your choice of recruitment method depends on your type of business, your location, and you. You have many sources available to you. A combination may serve your needs best. The important thing is to find the right applicant with the correct skills for the job you want to fill, whatever the source.

## Developing Applicants Forms

The hardest part of your work, if you did a good job listing the skills needed, is in finding and hiring the one right employee. You need some method of screening the applicants and selecting the best one for the position.

The application form is a tool which you can use to make your tasks of interviewing and selection easier. The form should have blank spaces for all the facts you need as a basis for judging the applicants. A sample form is provided below.

You will want a fairly complete application so you can get sufficient information. However, keep the form as simple as you can. The form may be mimeographed or ditto form.

Have the applicants fill out the application before you talk to them. It makes an excellent starting point for the interview. It is also a written record of experience and former employer's names and addresses.

Remember, the Civil Rights Act of 1964 prohibits discrimination in employment practices because of race, religion, sex, or national origin. Public Law 90-202 prohibits discrimination on the basis of age with respect to individuals who are at least 40 but less than 70. Federal laws also prohibit discrimination against the physically handicapped.

When an applicant has had work experience, other references are not very important. However, if the level of work experience is limited, additional references may be obtained from other individuals such as school counselors who can give objective information. Personal references are almost useless as an applicant would only list people who have a kind word for them.

## Interviewing Job Applicants

The objective of the job interview is to find out as much information as you can about the job applicant's work background, especially work habits and skills. Your major task is to get the applicants to talk about themselves and about their work habits. The best way to go about this is to ask each applicant specific questions: What did you do on your last job? How did you do it? Why was it done?

As you go along, evaluate the applicants' replies. Do they know what they are talking about? Are they evasive or unskilled in the job tasks? Can they account for discrepancies?

When the interview is over, ask the applicant to check back with you later, if you think you may be interested in that applicant. Never commit yourself until you have interviewed all likely applicants. You want to be sure that you select the right applicant for the job.

Next, verify the information you have obtained. A previous employer is usually the best source. Sometimes, a previous employer will give out information over the telephone. But it is usually best to request your information in writing and get a written reply.

To help insure a prompt reply, you should ask previous employers a few specific questions about the applicant which can be answered by a yes or no check, or with a very short answer. For example: How long did the employee work for you? _____ Was his or her work poor _____, average _____, or excellent _____ ? Why did the employee leave your employment?

After you have verified the information on all your applicants, you are ready to make your selection. The right employee can help you make money. The wrong employee will cost you much wasted time, materials, and may even drive away your customers.

## 4. Employee Training and Development

The quality of employees and their development through training and education are major factors in determining long-term profitability of a small business. If you hire and keep good employees, it is good policy to invest in the development of their skills, so they can increase their productivity.

Training often is considered for new employees only. This is a mistake because ongoing training for current employees helps them adjust to rapidly changing job requirements.

### Purpose of Training and Development

Reasons for emphasizing the growth and development of personnel include

Creating a pool of readily available and adequate replacements for personnel who may leave or move up in the organization.

Enhancing the company's ability to adopt and use advances in technology because of a sufficiently knowledgeable staff.

Building a more efficient, effective and highly motivated team, which enhances the company's competitive position and improves employee morale.

Ensuring adequate human resources for expansion into new programs.

Research has shown specific benefits that a small business receives from training and developing its workers, including:

Increased productivity.

Reduced employee turnover.

Increased efficiency resulting in financial gains.

Decreased need for supervision.

Employees frequently develop a greater sense of self-worth, dignity and well-being as they become more valuable to the firm and to society. Generally they will receive a greater share of the material gains that result from their increased productivity. These factors give them a sense of satisfaction through the achievement of personal and company goals.

**The Training Process**

The model below traces the steps necessary in the training process:

Organizational Objectives

Needs Assessment

Is There a Gap?

Training Objectives

Select the Trainees

Select the Training Methods and Mode

Choose a Means of Evaluating

Administer Training

Evaluate the Training

Your business should have a clearly defined strategy and set of objectives that direct and drive all the decisions made especially for training decisions. Firms that plan their training process are more successful than those that do not. Most business owners want to succeed, but do not engage in training designs that promise to improve their chances of success. Why? The five reasons most often identified are:

**Time** - Small businesses managers find that time demands do not allow them to train employees.

**Getting started** - Most small business managers have not practiced training employees. The training process is unfamiliar.

**Broad expertise** - Managers tend to have broad expertise rather than the specialized skills needed for training and development activities.

**Lack of trust and openness** - Many managers prefer to keep information to themselves. By doing so they keep information from subordinates and others who could be useful in the training and development process.

**Skepticism as to the value of the training** - Some small business owners believe the future cannot be predicted or controlled and their efforts, therefore, are best centered on current activities i.e., making money today.

A well-conceived training program can help your firm succeed. A program structured with the company's strategy and objectives in mind has a high probability of improving productivity and other goals that are set in the training mission.

For any business, formulating a training strategy requires addressing a series of questions.

Who are your customers? Why do they buy from you?

Who are your competitors? How do they serve the market? What competitive advantages do they enjoy? What parts of the market have they ignored?

What strengths does the company have? What weaknesses?

What social trends are emerging that will affect the firm?

The purpose of formulating a training strategy is to answer two relatively simple but vitally important questions: (1) What is our business? and (2) What should our business be? Armed with the answers to these questions and a clear vision of its mission, strategy and objectives, a company can identify its training needs.

## Identifying Training Needs

Training needs can be assessed by analyzing three major human resource areas: the organization as a whole, the job characteristics and the needs of the individuals. This analysis will provide answers to the following questions:

Where is training needed?

What specifically must an employee learn in order to be more productive?

Who needs to be trained?

Begin by assessing the current status of the company how it does what it does best and the abilities of your employees to do these tasks. This analysis will provide some benchmarks against which the effectiveness of a training program can be evaluated. Your firm should know where it wants to be in five years from its long-range strategic plan. What you need is a training program to take your firm from here to there.

Second, consider whether the organization is financially committed to supporting the training efforts. If not, any attempt to develop a solid training program will fail.

Next, determine exactly where training is needed. It is foolish to implement a companywide training effort without concentrating resources where they are needed most. An internal audit will help point out areas that may benefit from training. Also, a skills inventory can help determine the skills possessed by the employees in general. This inventory will help the organization determine what skills are available now and what skills are needed for future development.

Also, in today's market-driven economy, you would be remiss not to ask your customers what they like about your business and what areas they think should be improved. In summary, the analysis should focus on the total organization and should tell you (1) where training is needed and (2) where it will work within the organization.

Once you have determined where training is needed, concentrate on the content of the program. Analyze the characteristics of the job based on its description, the written narrative of what the employee actually does. Training based on job descriptions should go into detail about how the job is performed on a task-by-task basis.

Actually doing the job will enable you to get a better feel for what is done.

Individual employees can be evaluated by comparing their current skill levels or performance to the organization's performance standards or anticipated needs. Any discrepancies between actual and anticipated skill levels identifies a training need.

## Selection of Trainees

Once you have decided what training is necessary and where it is needed, the next decision is who should be trained? For a small business, this question is crucial. Training an employee is expensive, especially when he or she leaves your firm for a better job. Therefore, it is important to carefully select who will be trained.

Training programs should be designed to consider the ability of the employee to learn the material and to use it effectively, and to make the most efficient use of resources possible. It is also important that employees be motivated by the training experience. Employee failure in the program is not only damaging to the employee but a waste of money as well. Selecting the right trainees is important to the success of the program.

## Training Goals

The goals of the training program should relate directly to the needs determined by the assessment process outlined above. Course objectives should clearly state what behavior or skill will be changed as a result of the training and should relate to the mission and strategic plan of the company. Goals should include milestones to help take the employee from where he or she is today to where the firm wants him or her in the future. Setting goals helps to evaluate the training program and also to motivate employees. Allowing employees to participate in setting goals increases the probability of success.

## Training Methods

There are two broad types of training available to small businesses: on-the-job and off-the-job techniques. Individual circumstances and the "who," "what" and "why" of your training program

determine which method to use.

**On-the-job training** is delivered to employees while they perform their regular jobs. In this way, they do not lose time while they are learning. After a plan is developed for what should be taught, employees should be informed of the details. A timetable should be established with periodic evaluations to inform employees about their progress. On-the-job techniques include orientations, job instruction training, apprenticeships, internships and assistantships, job rotation and coaching.

**Off-the-job techniques** include lectures, special study, films, television conferences or discussions, case studies, role playing, simulation, programmed instruction and laboratory training. Most of these techniques can be used by small businesses although, some may be too costly.

**Orientations** are for new employees. The first several days on the job are crucial in the success of new employees. This point is illustrated by the fact that 60 percent of all employees who quit do so in the first ten days. Orientation training should emphasize the following topics:

The company's history and mission.

The key members in the organization.

The key members in the department, and how the department helps fulfill the mission of the company.

Personnel rules and regulations.

Some companies use verbal presentations while others have written presentations. Many small businesses convey these topics in one-on-one orientations. No matter what method is used, it is important that the newcomer understand his or her new place of employment.

**Lectures** present training material verbally and are used when the goal is to present a great deal of material to many people. It is more cost effective to lecture to a group than to train people individually. Lecturing is one-way communication and as such may not be the most effective way to train. Also, it is hard to ensure that the entire audience understands a topic on the same level; by targeting the average attendee you may undertrain some and lose others. Despite these drawbacks, lecturing is the most cost-effective way of reaching large audiences.

**Role playing and simulation** are training techniques that attempt to bring realistic decision making situations to the trainee. Likely problems and alternative solutions are presented for discussion. The adage there is no better trainer than experience is exemplified with this type of training. Experienced employees can describe real world experiences, and can help in and learn from developing the solutions to these simulations. This method is cost effective and is used in marketing and management training.

**Audiovisual methods** such as television, videotapes and films are the most effective means of providing real world conditions and situations in a short time. One advantage is that the presentation is the same no matter how many times it's played. This is not true with lectures, which can change as the speaker is changed or can be influenced by outside constraints. The major flaw with the audiovisual method is that it does not allow for questions and interactions with the speaker, nor does it allow for changes in the presentation for different audiences.

**Job rotation** involves moving an employee through a series of jobs so he or she can get a good feel for the tasks that are associated with different jobs. It is usually used in training for supervisory positions. The employee learns a little about everything. This is a good strategy for small businesses because of the many jobs an employee may be asked to do.

**Apprenticeships** develop employees who can do many different tasks. They usually involve several related groups of skills that allow the apprentice to practice a particular trade, and they take place over a long period of time in which the apprentice works for, and with, the senior skilled worker. Apprenticeships are especially appropriate for jobs requiring production skills.

**Internships and assistantships** are usually a combination of classroom and on-the-job training. They are often used to train prospective managers or marketing personnel.

**Programmed learning**, computer-aided instruction and interactive video all have one thing in common: they allow the trainee to learn at his or her own pace. Also, they allow material already learned to be bypassed in favor of material with which a trainee is having difficulty. After the introductory period, the instructor need not be present, and the trainee can learn as his or her time allows. These methods sound good, but may be beyond the resources of some small businesses.

**Laboratory training** is conducted for groups by skilled trainers. It usually is conducted at a neutral site and is used by upper- and middle management trainees to develop a spirit of teamwork and an increased ability to deal with management and peers. It can be costly and usually is offered by larger small businesses.

## Trainers

Who actually conducts the training depends on the type of training needed and who will be receiving it. On-the-job training is conducted mostly by supervisors; off-the-job training, by either in-house personnel or outside instructors.

In-house training is the daily responsibility of supervisors and employees. Supervisors are ultimately responsible for the productivity and, therefore, the training of their subordinates. These supervisors should be taught the techniques of good training. They must be aware of the knowledge and skills necessary to make a productive employee. Trainers should be taught to establish goals and objectives for their training and to determine how these objectives can be used to influence the productivity of their departments. They also must be aware of how adults learn and how best to communicate with adults. Small businesses need to develop their supervisors' training capabilities by sending them to courses on training methods. The investment will pay off in increased productivity.

There are several ways to select training personnel for off-the-job training programs. Many small businesses use in-house personnel to develop formal training programs to be delivered to employees off line from their normal work activities, during company meetings or individually at prearranged training sessions.

There are many outside training sources, including consultants, technical and vocational schools, continuing education programs, chambers of commerce and economic development groups. Selecting an outside source for training has advantages and disadvantages. The biggest advantage is that these organizations are well versed in training techniques, which is often not the case with in-house personnel.

The disadvantage of using outside training specialists is their limited knowledge of the company's product or service and customer needs. These trainers have a more general knowledge of customer satisfaction and needs. In many cases, the outside trainer can develop this knowledge quickly by immersing himself or herself in the company prior to training the employees. Another disadvantage of using outside trainers is the relatively high cost compared to in-house training, although the higher cost may be offset by the increased effectiveness of the training.

Whoever is selected to conduct the training, either outside or in-house trainers, it is important that the company's goals and values be carefully explained.

## Training Administration

Having planned the training program properly, you must now administer the training to the selected employees. It is important to follow through to make sure the goals are being met. Questions to consider before training begins include:

Location.

Facilities.

Accessibility.

Comfort.

Equipment.

Timing.

Careful attention to these operational details will contribute to the success of the training program.

An effective training program administrator should follow these steps:

Define the organizational objectives.

Determine the needs of the training program.

Define training goals.

Develop training methods.

Decide whom to train.

Decide who should do the training.

Administer the training.

Evaluate the training program.

Following these steps will help an administrator develop an effective training program to ensure that the firm keeps qualified employees who are productive, happy workers. This will contribute positively to the bottom line.

## Evaluation of Training

Training should be evaluated several times during the process. Determine these milestones when you develop the training. Employees should be evaluated by comparing their newly acquired skills with the skills defined by the goals of the training program. Any discrepancies should be noted and adjustments made to the training program to enable it to meet specified goals. Many training programs fall short of their expectations simply because the administrator failed to evaluate its progress until it was too late. Timely evaluation will prevent the training from straying from its goals.

## 5. Building Employee Trust

The most effective way to build trust in the workplace is to work together. There are no magic gimmicks or other simple solutions. Trust cannot be created by excessive wages, great company picnics or wonderful working conditions; it can only be generated through teamwork, honesty and fairness. Although trust and productivity are complex issues and represent only part of the total fabric of interpersonal relationships in small businesses, three attributes appear to have a positive effect on trust in successful small businesses:

The owner-manager of the small business is open and honest about the day-to-day business operations.

The owner-manager of the small business is consistent and fair about personnel policies.

The owner-manager spends a great deal of his or her time concentrating on good communications with those working in the firm.

### Honesty

Secrecy breeds suspicion. Whenever information is kept on close hold, the context becomes open to misinterpretation. Total quality improvement is based on the concept that workers care as much about the success of the small business as the owners do. Studies of small businesses indicate that employees tend to overestimate profits by substantial amounts. These same studies indicate that when true financial information is shared with employees, substantial cost controls are voluntarily initiated by all members of the work force.

Whenever in doubt concerning the amount of information to share with employees, experience indicates that too much is better than not enough. Never lie to workers about human relations issues. Institutional memory is long term; any deceit will be remembered for many years. Note that employees talk with each other and inconsistencies will be quickly detected and brought to the surface frequently to your embarrassment. The following are suggestions on how to avoid this dilemma:

Take time to talk with your workers.

Find out what they're thinking.

Find out what they'd like to know and tell them whenever possible.

Don't tell only good things.

Allow employees an opportunity to provide you, the owner, with information, questions and suggestions.

In this way, communications are two way.

**Fairness**

Fairness ranges from consistency in personnel actions and fair market practices to adherence to the various laws governing the workplace.

The concept of due process requires that a small business follow its own rules and policies. Employees must be treated the same when it comes to personnel issues.

Each worker should have an equal chance to perform at his or her best. Decisions concerning rewards, promotions and advancement should always be based on performance, and good performance should be spelled out in the job description. When performance is equal among employees, seniority should be used to break ties.

The key to healthy work relations is managing communications within the firm. Most of the communication will flow as orders and instructions to employees. Nevertheless, communicating (and honesty and fairness) is a two-way process. It is difficult for employees to be intelligent and enthusiastic teamworkers if they do not know the reasons behind orders and instructions. Perhaps even more important is giving employees the opportunity to contribute ideas and opinions before the manager-owner makes a decision. This adds dignity and meaning to the job in the eyes of most employees and their families.

Communicating includes telling employees where they stand, how the business is doing and what future plans are being developed. Negative feedback may be necessary at times, but positive feedback should be the primary tool for establishing good human relations. Never forget that employees are people, and that they will quickly detect insincerity. They also will respond to honest efforts to treat them as mature, responsible adults. Some practical human relations techniques that stimulate two-way communications include:

Periodic performance review sessions (every three months).

Bulletin boards.

Suggestion boxes.

Newsletters.

Regular open meetings.

## The Legal Environment

Small businesses operate in a complex legal environment that places many constraints on recruitment, selection, placement and other personnel practices. Laws may specify what is required, what is acceptable or what is prohibited. Every personnel system must consider the statutes relating to these issues.

The past years have been characterized by laws that encourage collective bargaining and that try to bring about a better balance between management and labor. Many of these laws apply to small businesses.

## The Personnel Manager

Many small businesses cannot afford a full-time specialist to deal with human resource problems. However, as a business grows, its structure becomes more complex and personnel problems increase in number and potential cost. At a certain point in the typical small business, it becomes apparent that a full-time or part-time personnel manager is needed. Conditions that indicate the necessity of a personnel manager include:

The firm has more than 100 employees.

Employees are represented by a union.

Turnover is very high (and costly).

The need for skilled or semiskilled labor creates problems

in recruitment or selection.

Employee morale is low.

Competition for good personnel is especially keen in the market area.

# 6. Productivity Improvement

It is conceivable for you to have more employees than the competition yet your company produces less and for you to have disgruntled, low-output employees even though you pay your employees more than the competition pays theirs. Productivity surveys and case studies indicate that increased worker motivation and satisfaction can increase worker output. Progressive, innovative managers now achieve productivity gains with human resource management techniques that go beyond pay incentives.

This Guide discusses how to increase worker output by motivating with quality of work life concepts and by tailoring benefits to meet the needs of employees. Cost: enlightened human resource management probably costs no more than employee turnover (hiring and training new employees), unwarranted pay increases, and low productivity. Benefit: better productivity; loyal, efficient workers; higher quality work, and increased likelihood of staying in business.

The essence of employee motivation and effectiveness is the manner in which they are managed. A direct relationship exists between effective management (i.e., providing a work environment that simultaneously achieves company goals and employees' goals) and modern human resource management.

Your management success is judged by your skill and knowledge in recognizing and assessing issues that concern employees and by your ability to resolve these concerns with employee help and satisfaction.

Do your employees know how you judge and measure their

performance?

Do you provide and encourage individual development with training and educational programs?

Do you trust your employees and rely upon their knowledge?

Do you let employees make decisions?

Do you have timely, accurate, open two-way communication with your employees?

If you answer no to all of these questions, you probably are an unsatisfactory human resource manager and have (or will have) employee-productivity problems.

## Quality of Work Life

Getting high quality job performance from your employees depends on giving employees opportunities for their personal growth, achievement, responsibility, recognition, and reward.

Pay - money - is the primary need and reward. Once the compensation (pay and benefits) is established properly, it is necessary to use other means to further motivate and improve your work force's output. The basis of all job enhancement efforts is your recognition of employees' desire to do good work, to assume responsibility, to achieve and to succeed.

Changes to consider in creating a new quality of work life atmosphere include:

**From:** detailed job descriptions with specific tasks and rigid instruction for how to do the work

**To:** Flexible, diverse work assignment allowing self-regulation, variety and challenge;

**From:** Structured chain of command, managers making decisions and supervisors bossing

**To:** Worker involvement in planning, decision making and operating procedure;

**From:** Hierarchical channels of communications;

**To:** Direct, fast two-way communication

**From:** Limited on-the-job instruction

**To:** Advanced training, educational and career development opportunities;

**From:** Job specialization in one task

**To:** Leeway allowed for every employee to complete many task by crossing lines of specialization;

**From:** Obscure, irregular job evaluations

**To:** Objective job performance standards with measures fairly administered;

**From:** Careless or neglected safety and health conditions;

**To:** Clean, safe and healthful working conditions.

The quality of work life technique is to involve your employees by sharing the management responsibility and authority with them - the workers who do the job.

## Flexible Benefits

Compensation costs - salaries, wages, and benefits - are a large and increasing part of operating expenses; yet, productivity can decline among workers who get more pay and benefits. Workers are productive with fair pay tied to performance. Ironically, not all employee motivation and productivity problems are solved by pay raises and promotions. It isn't necessary to make pay adjustments beyond a fair industry-wide (market place) level.

The tailoring of benefits to satisfy specific needs is part of the quality of work life technique. It is a way to maximize the amount of labor costs going to the employee and to maximize your return on these costs without increasing across-the-board expenses. By making a special effort to satisfy individual employee needs, you reinforce the motivational value of the flexible benefit.

For example, you can reduce unwanted employee turnover and related recruiting, hiring, and training costs by shifting these costs from developing new employees to keeping experienced employees. You can motivate an employee to increase productivity by providing opportunities for career development (training or schooling).

At the same time you have improved the worker's skills and shown recognition of the worker's value and aspiration. A tailored benefit can be worth as much to an employee as a pay raise. Such a benefit is practical because (1) it probably costs no more than worker unrest and diminished productivity and (2) it is probably less costly than a comparable pay increase.

Age, education, job experience, job fulfillment, marital status, and family size are considerations that determine the utility and attractiveness of a benefit. Different benefits appeal to different people. Everyone's needs are different. A younger employee might be motivated by having use of a company car. An older person may want more status like a title or a professional association membership. The list of possible employees benefits and their applications is nearly unlimited. To get the maximum value, you've got to tailor the benefit to the job and your business requirements and financial capability.

**Think how you could use:**

pre-tax thrift-savings programs

recreational programs

discounts

scholarships

personal financial planning

loans

tuition refund

profit sharing

company car

personal expense account

parking privileges

legal assistance

extra vacation

child care

job titles

professional or trade association memberships

travel

A flexible benefit is two-fold. Not only does the benefit satisfy some employee's specific need but it also communicates your concern to meet these needs, creating the kind of work environment that contributes to increased employee productivity.

You must recognize the productivity problem and the needs of your employees so that you can tailor the benefit to meet the situation. Beyond pay and statutory benefits that provide the most value to your business.

## Salary Compression

Ralph is an experienced employee. You think he is good but he is complaining that his salary is not enough. You're puzzled and angry because you gave him a raise and a cost of living increase a month ago and the salary is competitive. Ralph seems ungrateful and his output is down. After talking with Ralph, you learn that he feels he should be paid more than Ed, a new employee. You hired Ralph two years ago at $62,000, a year. He's now making $68,500. But Ed, was just hired at $56,000. Ralph thinks he should have more to show for his two years experience compared to Ed, who is younger with no experience.

You realize that starting salaries have gone up at a faster rate than regular pay increases. Attracting educated employees was competitive. Result: the difference in pay got smaller between experienced and less experienced employees. This is called salary compression.

Your experienced employees don't like it. They will react negatively, slowing down and looking for another job, another promotion, or another raise. In this situation you could recognize Ralph's experience, tenure and value with flexible benefits.

Using quality of work life techniques to motivate and to reward employees can result in productivity gains. The ultimate goal, of course, is to achieve the maximum result from the least effort, the greatest profit for the least cost, the largest output from the smallest input. To work toward this goal you've got to know how productive your company is. Thus, you must define and measure productivity for comparison from time to time.

**Productivity Measurement**

Definitions of and ways to measure productivity vary. A basic way to express productivity is productivity equals output divided by input i.e., productivity is the ratio of output to input, or simply output over input. The quantity of output is measured in units produced, dollars of sales, or any term that suits your need. The quality of output is measured by workmanship, adherence to standard, and absence of complaints. Input is measured by labor costs, hours worked, and number of employees. To be useful, measures must be as simple and as consistent as possible.

A simple and understandable method of productivity measurement is to divide total sales (output in dollars) by total compensation costs (input). Increases and prices are accounted for automatically; however, you must adjust for inflation. To compare productivity measures in different years, pick a base year and give it an index of 100. Then figure your ratio of compensation to sales and with that number calculate the index and compare the fluctuation of the indexes.

Using output over input, you can measure any activity and employee. A typist's productivity can be measured in terms of numbers of pages typed, a salesperson by number of customer calls or amount of sales. When deciding how and what to measure, consider what a person does, how well, how much, and how often.

The indexes measure the productivity increases and decreases that indicate changes in your company's performance. You need these measures so that you

1)  can set goals and priorities,

2)  know where you stand,

3)  are motivated by objective reasons - by numbers, not subjective feelings, and

4)  have a common basis of communication with employees, bankers and consultants.

**Chancing the Change**

For many, if not most, companies adoption of quality of work life and flexible benefits management techniques can dramatically change how things are done. It is difficult and risky to make these changes; however, such changes may be not only necessary but also the difference between companies that are competitive and companies that aren't. Experience shows that with proper consultation, planning, training, and implementation the innovative human resource management concept is becoming the standard for effective management.

## 7. Delegating Work and Responsibility

Delegating work, responsibility, and authority is difficult in a company because it means letting others make decisions which involve spending the owner-manager's money. At a minimum, you should delegate enough authority to get the work done, to allow assistants to take initiative, and to keep the operation moving in your absence.

This Guide discusses controlling those who carry responsibility and authority and coaching them in self-improvement. It emphasizes the importance of allowing competent assistants to perform in their own style rather than insisting that things be done exactly as the owner-manager would personally do them.

"Let others take care of the details."

That, in a few words, is the meaning of delegating work and responsibility.

In theory, the same principles for getting work done through other people apply whether you have 25 employees and one top assistant or 150 to 200 employees and several managers. Yet, putting the principles into practice is often difficult.

Delegation is perhaps the hardest job owner-managers have to learn. Some never do. They insist on handling many details and work themselves into early graves. Others pay lip service to the idea but actually run a one-man shop. They give their assistants many responsibilities but little or no authority.

## How Much Authority?

Authority is the fuel that makes the machine go when you delegate work and responsibility. It poses a question: To what extent do you allow another person to make decisions which involve spending your company's money?

That question is not easy to answer. Sometimes, an owner-manager has to work it out as he goes along, as did Tom Brasser. His pride in being the top man made it hard for him to share authority. He tried, but he found to his dismay that his delegating was not as good as he thought.

One day when he returned from his first short business trip. Mr. Brasser stormed out of his office. He waved a sheaf of payroll sheets and shouted "Who approved all this overtime while I was away?" I did," the production chief answered.

Realizing that all heads were turned to see what the shouting was about., Mr. Brasser lowered his voice. Taking the production manager with him, he stepped into his office.

There he told the production man, "You've got your nerve authorizing overtime. This is still my company, and I'll decide what extra costs we'll take on. You know good and well that our prices are not based on paying overtime rates."

"Right," the production man replied. "But you told me I was in full charge of production. You said I should keep pushing so I wouldn't fall behind on deliveries."

"That's right," Mr. Brasser said. "In fact, I recall writing you about a couple of orders just before I went out of town."

"You can say that again. And one of them - the big order - was getting behind so I approved overtime."

"I would have done the same thing if I has been here," Mr. Brasser said. "But let's get things straight for the future. From now on, overtime needs my okay. We've got to keep costs in line."

Mr. Brasser then followed up with his other department heads, including his office manager and purchasing agent. He called them in, told them what had happened, and made it clear that their authority did not include making decisions that would increase the company's operating costs. Such decisions had to have his approval, he pointed out, because it was his company. He was the one who would lose, if and when, increased costs ate up the profit.

Yet, if an owner-manager is to run a successful company, you must delegate authority properly. How much authority is proper depends on your situation.

At a minimum, you should delegate enough authority:

(1) To get the work done,

(2) To allow key employees to take initiative, and

(3) To keep things going in your absence.

## To Whom Do You Delegate?

Delegation of responsibility does not mean that you say to your assistants, "Here, you run the shop." The people to whom you delegate responsibility and authority must be competent in the technical areas for which you hold them accountable. However, technical competence is not enough.

In addition, the person who fills a key management spot in the organization must either be a manager or be capable of becoming one. A manager's chief job is to plan, direct, and coordinate the work of others.

A manager should possess the three "I's" - initiative, interest, and imagination. The manager of a department must have enough self-drive to start and keep things moving. A manager should not have to be told, for example, to make sure that employees start work on time.

Personality traits must be considered. A key manager should be strong- willed enough to overcome opposition when necessary and should also have enough ego to want to "look good" but not so much that it antagonizes other employees.

## Spell Out the Delegation

Competent people want to know for what they are being held responsible. The experience of Charles P. Wiley illustrates how one owner-manager let them know. He started by setting up an organization. He broke his small company into three departments: a production department, a sales department, and an administrative department.

The manager who handled production was responsible for advertising, customer solicitations, and customer service. Mr. Wiley regarded the administrative department as the headquarters and service unit for the other two. Its manager was responsible for personnel, purchasing, and accounting.

Mr. Wiley also worked out with his assistants the practices and procedures necessary to get the jobs done. His assistants were especially helpful in pointing out any overlaps or gaps in assigned responsibilities. He then put the procedures into writing. Thus each supervisor had a detailed statement of the function of each's department and the extent of each's authority.

This statement included a list of specific actions which they could take on their own initiative and a list of actions which required approval in the front office - Mr. Wiley, or in his absence, the assistant general manager.

Mr. Wiley had thought about the times when he might be absent from the plant. To make sure that things would keep moving, the production manager was designated assistant general manager and given authority to make all operational decisions in Mr. Wiley's absence.

In thinking about absences, Mr. Wiley went one step further. He instructed each department head to designate and train an assistant who could run the department if, and when, the need arose.

When you spell out the delegation, be sure that departments are coordinated. The experience of another small plant owner, Ann Jones, is a case in point. She thought her departments were coordinated until the shop manager reported that he was swamped with "rush" orders.

"It's impossible for me to make good on Bill's promise," the shop chief said. Bill was the sales manager.

When Bill was called in, he said "I had to promise early delivery to get the business."

Ms. Jones resolved the problem by instructing the sales manager and the shop manager to work out delivery dates together.

Make sure that departments are coordinated when you spell out the responsibilities and authority of each key manager. Thus you reduce the
chances of confusion as well as assuring that there is no doubt about who is responsible for specific jobs. Then, the particular key manager can take corrective action before things get out of hand.

## Keeping Control

When you manage through others, it is essential that you keep control. You do it by holding a subordinate responsible for his or her actions and checking the results of those actions.

In controlling your assistants, try to strike a balance. You should not get into a key manager's operation so closely that you stifle him or her should you be so far removed that you lose control of things.

You need feedback to keep yourself informed. Reports provide a way to get the right kind of feedback at the right time. They can be daily, weekly, or monthly, depending on how soon you need the information. Each department head can report his or her progress, or the lack of it, in the unit of production that is appropriate for his or her activity; for example, items packed in the shipping room, sales per territory, hours of work per employee.

Periodic staff meetings are another way to get feedback. At these meetings, department heads can comment on their activities, accomplishments, and problems.

## Coaching Your Staff

For the owner-manager, delegation does not end with good control. It involves coaching as well, because management ability is not acquired automatically. You have to teach it.

Just as important, you have to keep your managers informed just as you would be if you were doing their jobs. Part of your job is to see that they get the facts they need for making their decisions.

You should be certain that you convey your thinking when you coach your assistants. Sometimes words can be inconsistent with your thoughts. Ask questions to make sure the listener understands your meanings. In other words, delegation can only be effective when you have good communications.

And above all, listen. Many owner-managers get so involved in what they are saying or are going to say next, that they do not listen to the other person. In coaching a person so he or she can improve, it is important to tell why you give the instruction. When a person knows the reason, he or she is better able to supervise.

## Allow Staff to Work

Sometimes you find yourself involved in many operational details even though you do everything that is necessary for delegating responsibility. In spite of defining authority, delegating to competent persons, spelling out the delegation, keeping control, and coaching, you are still burdened with detailed work. Why? Usually, you have failed to do one vital things. You have refused to stand back and let the wheels turn.

If you are to make delegation work, you must allow your managers freedom to do things their way. You and the company are in trouble if you try to measure your assistants by whether or not they do a particular task exactly as you would do it. They should be judged by their results - not their methods.

No two persons react exactly the same in every situation. Be prepared to see some action taken differently from the way in which you would do it even though your policies are well defined. Of course, if an assistant strays too far from policy, you need to bring him or her back into line. You cannot afford second-guessing.

You should also keep in mind that when an owner-manager second-guesses assistants, you risk destroying their self-confidence. If the assistant does not run his or her department to your satisfaction and if his or her department to your satisfaction and if his or her shortcomings cannot be overcome, then replace that person. But when results prove his or her effectiveness, it is good practice to avoid picking at each move he or she makes.

## 8. Setting Up a Pay System

Pay administration is a management tool that enables you to control personnel cost, increase employee morale, and reduce workforce turnover. A formal pay system provides a means of rewarding individuals for their contributions to the success of your firm, while making sure that your organization receives a fair return on its investment in employee pay.

this guide provides time-tested concepts for determining competitive pay levels and for maintaining fair pay relationships among the jobs comprised by a small company.

### Who needs a pay administration plan?

Pay administration may just be a fancy term for something you are already doing but haven't bothered to name. Or, perhaps your organization has not been paying employees according to any system, but waiting until unrest shows up to make pay adjustments - using payroll to put out fires, so to speak.

A formal pay plan, one that lets employees know where they stand and where they can go as far as take home money are concerned, won't solve all your employee relations problems. It will, however, remove one of those areas of doubt and rumor that may keep your workforce anxious and unhappy and less loyal and more mobile than you'd like them to be.

What's in it for you? Let's face it, in business - particularly small business - it's good people who can make the difference between go and no go. Many people like a mystery, but not when it's about how their pay is set.

Employees under a pay plan they know and understand can see that it's equitable (fair) and equable (uniform) that pay isn't set by whim. They know what to expect and what they can hope to shoot for. In the long run such a plan can help you:

recruit employees

keep employees

motivate employees

It can help you build a solid foundation for a successful business.

## Developing and Installing the plan

A formal pay plan doesn't have to cost you a lot of time and money. Formal doesn't mean complex. In fact, the more elaborate the plan is, the more difficult it is to put into practice, communicate, and carry out.

the foremost concern in setting up a formal pay administration plan is to get the acceptance, understanding, and support of your management and supervisory employees. A well-defined, thoroughly discussed, and properly-understood plan is a prerequisite for success.

the steps in setting up a pay plan are:1) define the jobs, 2) evaluate the jobs, 3) price the jobs. 4) install the plan, communicate the plan to employees, and 6) appraise employee performance under the plan.

## Defining the Jobs

Unless you know each job's specifications and requirements, you can't compare them for pay purposes.

It's no surprise, therefore, that the initial step in installing a formal plan is preparing a job description for each position.

You may be able to write these descriptions yourself, since in many small businesses the owner-manager at one time or another has worked at just about every job. However, the best and easiest way to put together such job information is simply to ask employees to describe their jobs. Supervisors should be asked to review these descriptions.

Your best bet here is to prepare a simple form to be filled out by the employee (or someone interviewing the employee). This is the time to begin explaining to employees what you are doing. They need to know that their help is needed to develop the pay plan - that you are not trying to find out how well they are doing their jobs - just what they do. The form should contain the following categories:

**Job Title**

**Reporting Relationship**

**Specifications**

**Primary function** (What is the main responsibility of the job?)

Main Duties (List main duties in order of importance and estimate the percentage of time spent on each)

**Other Duties** (List of duties not performed on a regular basis.)

**Job Requirements:**

Formal Education or Training Required

Experience or Background Required

Technical/Administrative Complexity

Responsibility for Results

Responsibility for Supervision

Unusual Working Conditions

It will probably take some time to prepare job descriptions from the information you get from your employees, but what you learn may have other uses besides comparing jobs for pay purposes. For one thing, you may discover that some employees are not doing what you though they were, or what they were hired to do. You may find you want to make some changes in their work routines. The information may also be useful for:

Hiring, training, and developing employees;

Realigning duties in the organization;

Comparing job data for salary surveys;

Assuring compliance with various employment practice and pay rate laws; and

Evaluating job performance based on assigned duties.

## Evaluating the Jobs

Nobody knows a scientific, precise way of deciding exactly how much a particular job is worth to a company. Human judgment is the only way to put a dollar value on work. A good job evaluation method for firms with 100 or fewer employees is simple-ranking. It's a guess, too, but a pretty well controlled guess.

Under the simple-ranking system, job descriptions are compared against each other. They are ranked according to difficulty and responsibility. Using your judgment, you end up with an array of jobs that shows the relative value of each position to the company.

After you have ranked the job descriptions by value to the firm, the next step is to group jobs that are similar in scope and responsibility into the same pay grade. Then you arrange these groups in a series of pay levels from highest to lowest. The number of pay levels depends on the total number of jobs and types of work in your organization, but for a company with 100 or fewer jobs,10 or 12 pay levels is usually about right.

## Pricing the Jobs

So far in establishing a pay system, you've had to look only inside the company itself. To put a dollar value on each of your pay levels, you should look outside at the going rates for similar work in your area. Since you have ranked and grouped jobs in pay levels, you won't have to survey each job. Survey those in each level that are easiest to describe and are most common in local industry. Do try, however, to survey those jobs that have more than one level, for example junior and senior typists.

A survey of who's paying how much for what in your Locality is the best way of finding out how much you ought to pay for each of your jobs. You probably have neither the time nor the money to spend on making such a survey yourself. That shouldn't be a problem; you should be able to get all the data you need from sources such as your local

Chamber of Commerce, major firms located in your area, or from government agencies. If you belong to a trade association, you may be able to get its help to find out what the going rate is for one or more jobs in each pay level.

In studying pay in your area and applying what you learn to your own jobs, make sure you compare job descriptions, not just job titles. Job titles can be misleading; there can be great differences between what one organization and another call their jobs. One firm's janitor may be somebody else's environmental control engineer.

After you are satisfied that you are comparing apples and apples, you can compute an average rate (the averages in the guide are purely arbitrary) for each job and enter it on a worksheet as follows:

**Pay Level Position Average Rate**

1 Clerk-typist 974

2 Stenographer 1135

3 Payroll Clerk 1287

4 Secretary 1323

Accounting Clerk 1380

5 Computer Operator 1460

(and so on)

You may need to adjust the average rates somewhat to keep a sufficient difference between pay levels to separate them. The going rates you find for each pay level can then become the midpoints of your pay level ranges. (You can, of course, set your midpoints above or below the survey averages, based on your company's ability to pay, the length of your work week, and the type and value of your company's benefit programs.)

Typically, the minimum rate in a level is 85 percent of the midpoint rate, and the maximum rate is 115 percent of the midpoint. With this arrangement, a new employee can increase his or her earnings by 35 percent without a job change; thus having performance incentives even if he or she is not promoted.

You now have a pay range for each position in your organization. Such a pay range will enable you to tell where your employees' pay and pay potential stand in relation to the market rates for their kinds of work. It should show you at a glance where you need to make changes to achieve rates that are fair within your organization and pay that's competitive with similar businesses in your community.

In general, with a planned pay structure you should be able to tie individual rates of pay to job performance and contribution to company goals. It should also provide enough flexibility to handle special situations.

## Installing the plan

At this point you have the general plan, but you don't of course, pay in general. You pay each employee individually. You must now consider how the plan will be administered to provide for individual pay increases.

In administering the pay increase feature of the plan, you can use several approaches:

Merit increases, granted to recognize performance and contribution;

Promotion increases for employees assigned to different jobs in higher pay levels;

Progression to minimum for employees who are below the minimum or hiring rate for the pay level;

Probationary increases of newer employees who have attained the necessary skills and experience to function effectively;

Tenure increases for time with the company; and

General increases, granted employees to maintain real earnings as economic factors require and to keep pay competitive.

These approaches are the most common, but there are many variations. Most annual increases are made for cost of living, tenure, or employment market reasons. Obviously, you might use several, all, or combinations of the various increase methods.

You may find that a form for documenting salary increases and recording the reasons for them can be quite useful. You will probably find that records such as these are useful references for pay administration purposes.

## Telling employees about the plan

After you have set your pay administration plan into place, you have to consider how to tell employees about it. If setting up a good program is number one in importance, a close number two is explaining that plan to employees.

How to tell them is your decision. Some of the more successful methods include personal letters to each employee and meetings to explain the plan and answer question.

However you tell employees, you must clearly, honestly, and openly explain the way the plan works. This is a prime opportunity for you to build goodwill and good relations with your employees. Be sure your supervisors understand and can explain the plan to their people. Explaining the plan to new hires is also essential, and it's a good idea to review the plan periodically with all employees.

## Employee performance appraisal

The majority of employees in the labor force are under merit increase pay system, though most of their pay increases result from other factors. This approach involves periodic review and appraisal of how well employees perform their assigned duties. An effective employee appraisal plan:

Achieve better two-way communications between the manager and the employee,

Relates pay to work performance and results,

Provides a standardized approach to evaluating performance, and

Helps employees see how they can improve by helping them understand job responsibilities and expectations.

Such a performance review helps not only the employee whose work is being appraised, but also helps the manager doing the appraising to gain insight into the organization.

An open exchange between employee and manager can show the manager where improvements in equipment, procedures, or other factors might improve employee performance. Try to foster a climate in which employees can discuss progress and problems informally at any time throughout the year.

Again, to get the best results it's a good idea to use a form for appraisal. A typical form includes such job performance factors as:

Results achieved,

Quality of performance,

Volume of work,

Effectiveness in working with others in firm,

Effectiveness in dealing with customers, suppliers, etc.,

Initiative,

Job knowledge, and

Dependability.

You can design your own form, using examples you can find in books on personnel administration, if necessary. Your forms should be tailored to the jobs and should follow from your job analyses.

**How can the plan help you?**

The best pay plan in the world for employees won't be of any use if it doesn't help your business. What's in it for you?

Again, the answer is getting, keeping, and encouraging good employees. Your pay plan will help you:

**Recruit** - The pay ranges will provide competitive hiring rates for attracting high caliber employees.

**Retain** - The performance appraisal plan and pay increase feature will encourage performance plus growth and development within your organization.

**Motivate** - The pay plan will provide something to shoot for to keep employees interested in and enthusiastic about their present assignments and also provide the incentive to seek greater opportunity within your company.

Having capable employees who are interested and enthusiastic will help you win the battle for business survival and growth.

## Updating the plan

To keep your pay administration plan in tune with the times, you should review it at least annually. Make adjustments where necessary and don't forget to retrain supervisory personnel. This isn't the kind of plan that can be set up and then forgotten.

During your annual review, ask yourself if the plan is working for you. That's the most important question. Are you getting the kind of employees you want or are you just making do? What's the turnover rate? Do employees seem to care about the business? In the last analysis, it's not how elegant the plan is or how beautiful the forms and administration. What matters is how the plan helps you to achieve the objectives of your business.

# 9. Importance of Employee Relations

Carol Corcoran, who manages a deli, was heard complaining one day, "What am I going to do about help these days? I hire two young ladies to work behind the counter, and less than one week after they begin working, Lori starts asking for time off so she can go to the shore with her boy friend. How can I give her time off, without being unfair to the other girl? I certainly can't afford to give both girls time off."

In another town, George Zimmerman who manages a small asphalt plant was having more serious problems. "The last time Joe and Bill came they complained about the shop conditions - too sloppy and dirty - I had everybody clean up and we have kept the place cleaner since then. Now they want the walls painted. I can't do that; the next thing they'll want is air-conditioning. You can't satisfy people nowadays."

Both these situations involve personnel policies and the types of decisions which every owner/manager has to make.

This section should help you to improve your personnel policies so that you will have a more effective work force. Specifically it should help you:

Improve your personnel administration procedures

Improve the human relations practices, including the way projects are delegated

Assure positive and effective discipline

Enhance your ability to prevent employee grievances and

to handle those that do arise

Establish improved lines of communication as a foundation for higher employee morale

There are many ways to manage people. The manager can be strict or rigidly enforce rules. Communications can be one-way from boss to employee. The job might get done, but with fairly high turnover, absenteeism and low morale.

Or the owner can make an extra effort to be a "nice guy" to everyone on the payroll. This may lead to reduced adherence to the rules, and employees may argue when they are asked to do work they do not like. Controlling the daily operation of the business may become more and more difficult. The business may survive, but only with much lower profit than if the owner followed more competent personnel policies.

But there is another way. A way where employees can feel a part of your business, where manager and employee can communicate effectively with each other, where rules are fair and flexible, yet enforced with positive discipline. The job gets done efficiently and profitably, and the business does well.

People are your most important asset. What is the dollar-and-cents value of good working relations with your staff? Have you calculated what percentage your payroll is of total operating expenses? What are the costs of selecting, training, and replacing your employees? What labor turnover is the result of employee dissatisfaction? In terms of the output and the growth of your business, what is the real money value to you of a highly motivated and loyal work force?

Looking carefully at the answers to questions like these can help you develop a sound employee relations program.

Large companies have a separate personnel department. Most managers of a small business view this "personnel function" as just part of the general job of running a business. It is good practice, though, to think of your personnel function as a distinct and separate part of your responsibilities - only then will you give your personnel responsibilities the priorities they deserve.

The personnel function is generally considered to include all those policies and administrative procedures necessary to satisfy the needs of employees. Not necessarily in priority order, these include:

1. Administrative personnel procedures.

2. Supervisory practices based on human relations and competent delegation.

3. Positive discipline.

4. Grievance prevention and grievance handling.

5. A system of communications.

## 10. Administrative Personnel Procedures

Favorable employee relations require competent handling of the administrative aspects of the personnel function. These include the management of:

Work hours

The physical working environment:

Facilities

Equipment

Payroll procedures

benefit procedures, including insurance matters, and vacation and holiday schedules

### Work Hours

Work hours must meet the needs of the business but should also be flexible enough to take the personal needs of each employee into account. For example, it may be possible to set business hours from 8:00 a.m. to 6:00 p.m., and allow most people to choose any regular work day within those hours. It may not even be necessary for everyone to work the same total hours per week. You might let some employees work a shorter week to fill peak loads or to keep the business open for more than eight hours a day. In any case, allowing some flexibility in working hours will not only result in increased employee satisfaction, but will likely lead to greater productivity as well.

No matter how flexible working hours are, however, it is important that each employee understand the hours to be worked. Often a simple chart of names and work hours is all that is needed to assure that everyone knows at a glance, who is working when.

## The Physical Working Environment

Conditions of facilities and equipment can greatly affect the attitudes of employees. The temperature, lighting and cleanliness in and around the working area and the general maintenance of equipment are all important to an employee's satisfaction on the job. Even a draft or a cold floor can make a difference in a person's perception of you as a good employer.

Employees need facilities for lunch, especially if there are no restaurants in the area. Good employee practices suggest that a refrigerator, a sink, and even a small employee lunch area for breaks and lunch hours should be available.

Clean toilet facilities and a personal locker or adequate closet space for clothing of employees are a necessity. Parking arrangements are also important. When an employee comes to work and finds no parking place, and has to look for one, possibly for some time, he or she will not start the day ready for high achievement. When it is necessary to ask employees to park fairly far away - such as in a shopping mall where the better parking spaces have to be reserved for customers, the need for this inconvenience should be clearly explained to employees when they are first hired.

Fairness in assigning people to equipment, or equipment to people is another important procedural matter which affects the satisfaction your people gain from their work. It is no slight matter if the new vehicle or the new computer is assigned carelessly, without good reason.

Individually, each of these aspects of working conditions can be significant sources of complaints and even grievances. Together they have great influence on the work climate that exists in your firm. Unless you consider all of them seriously, and keep the needs of your employees in mind, your employees will feel that you have little regard for their physical well-being.

## Payroll Procedures

Wages and salaries are such important matters to employees that it is not only important to pay fairly, but also promptly and accurately.

People want to receive their pay when they have been told to expect it. Your staff reacts favorably, not only to prompt payment, but to the immediate correction of any errors that may have occurred. Employees are rightfully annoyed if their legitimate requests are treated as impositions. Cheerful attention to such problems will generally be appreciated especially if it is clear evidence of a spirit of concern for the employee's welfare. An opportunity to show such concern presents itself every so often when a minor emergency will force someone to ask for his or her pay a day or two early. If it is at all possible, and the emergency is valid, it brings goodwill to satisfy such a request. When such exceptions are granted, however, it should be made clear, in a nice way, that they cannot become regular practice.

## Benefit Procedures

A benefits program brings the best results when employees who have claims are helped with filing them and if someone follows up when an insurance company does not process the claim promptly. Information on benefits should, of course, be provided to employees, from time to time.

Vacation time, too, is important to employees. Some have to coordinate with spouses, others take advantage of special travel offers or other opportunities. As much as possible, good personnel policies require that vacation schedules are prepared early during the year so employees who want to make plans find out whether their preferred dates are available. You can, of course, specify that you will close certain weeks or that, at all times, certain positions have to be covered (two salespeople have to be on the floor at all times, or someone has to be in the shop who can weld, or someone has to cover the telephone, etc.).

To prevent conflicts from affecting business performance, it should be understood how they will be resolved - by who asked for a date first or by seniority or some other way.

What applies to vacations also applies to holidays, to some extent. Your company's paid holidays should be well known to the entire staff of course. Here, too, flexibility could be used. If you are in a business which is open during some holidays, schedules should be prepared far in advance so everyone knows who is expected to work and who will have the day off. If your business can be flexible, it is a good idea to let people shift holidays if they would prefer to do so, or even allow them to work and earn an extra day's pay. Here, as in all other personnel functions, it is better to adopt flexible policies which give great freedom to employees to satisfy personal needs. With such flexibility in the personnel function, a business can be much more insistent that rules and work standards be adhered to. This is a fair arrangement. In personnel policies, the company tries to do the best possible to adapt to the needs and expectations of people. In return, employees are expected to honor the company's need for reliability, adherence to reasonable rules, schedules and work standards - all of which have to be clearly communicated by words and deeds.

## 11. Effective Supervisory Practices

If an employee's job satisfies his or her needs, the employee responds more favorably to the job. This may happen, for example, when an employee is given the responsibility for managing the office on his or her own, and is recognized for doing it well. Or it may occur when a sales representative is assigned full responsibility for developing new business as well as maintaining existing customers in a territory and is recognized for the accomplishment. Such employees tend to take their responsibilities seriously, act positively for the firm, and are absent from work only rarely.

The key point is that when a job satisfies needs, the employee may bring greater commitment to the job. Some needs common to all individuals are basics like food, shelter, and security for the future. Normally a fair wage level and a feeling of security that the job will continue, tend to satisfy these needs. Such needs, however, can be satisfied in most jobs today, and they do not alone evoke heavy commitment by employees to your firm.

Other needs must also be satisfied. Most of these are related to:

a. The firm's personnel practices such as complaint handling or vacation scheduling

b. Working conditions

c. Supervisory practices such as discipline, or the way instructions are given, and

d. Total compensation, including benefits practices.

If what the firm provides in any of these aspects is seen by the employees as much poorer than what other firms in the area provide, dissatisfactions will result. On the other hand, improvements above an acceptable level generally do not bring about greater employee commitment in the long run.

For example, total disregard for employee complaints (personnel practices) can lead to serious problems for the firm. When employee complaints are handled well, serious problems tend to be precluded from developing but there is no major gain in deep employee commitment to the job.

What then does bring about a serious commitment to the job and firm?

There are five factors that generally cause a deep commitment to job performance for most employees. These are:

**1. The work itself** - to what extent does the employee see the work as meaningful and worthwhile?

**2. Achievement** - how much opportunity is there for the employee to accomplish tasks that are seen as a reasonable challenge?

**3. Responsibility** - to what extent does the employee have assignment and the authority necessary to take care of a significant function of the organization?

**4. Recognition** - to what extent is the employee aware of how highly other people value the contributions made by the employee?

**5. Advancement** - how much opportunity is there for the employee to assume greater responsibilities in the firm?

These five factors tend to satisfy certain critical needs of individuals:

One need is the feeling of being accepted as part of the firm's work-team.

Another need is for feeling important - that the employee's strengths, capabilities and contributions are known and valued highly.

A third need is for the chance to continue to grow and become a more fully functioning person.

If the kinds of needs just described are met by paying attention to the five factors previously listed, an owner/manager will have taken significant steps toward gaining the full commitment of employees to job performance. To do this, several practical strategies can be used, such as:

Establishing confidence and trust with your employees through open communication and the development of sensitivity to employee needs

Allowing employees participation in decision-making which directly affects them

Helping employees to set their own work methods and work goals, as much as possible

Praising and rewarding good work as clearly and promptly as inadequate performance is mentioned

Restructuring jobs to be challenging and interesting by

giving increased responsibilities and independence to those who want it, and who can handle it

## Good Delegation

One practical way to work on these strategies is to practice good delegation.

Simply defined, delegation is the granting of authority and independence to another person to complete a project. It must be understood that with the authority to do a job, comes the responsibility to get it done.

A manager who practices good delegation automatically also makes use of the strategies which bring greater commitment on their part.

A second benefit of good delegation - one not related to the personnel functions - lies in the opportunity it gives you to spend more of your time on important work which you cannot delegate.

For all these reasons, delegating work and responsibility can be very beneficial to you and for your company. But to be effective, delegation must be used with some caution. Before delegating a project, you, as the manager, must first answer two questions:

1. To whom should projects be delegated?

2. What kind and how much work and responsibility can be delegated to this person?

It is important to understand that delegation involves projects which include significant decision making. If your employee is not given the responsibility to make decisions, it is not delegation. The assigning of routine and repetitive work does not bring the benefits which delegation can bring and therefore is not part of the strategy for achieving a climate that brings greater commitment by employees.

Work assignment, even though the employee is asked to perform a specific task as assigned, also has the potential to add to the positive climate - when it is fair and takes employee preferences into consideration This, obviously, is difficult to do all the time, but if employees are given as much of a voice in deciding who should receive non-regular work assignments, good ones as well as undesirable ones, then these assignments are likely to have a beneficial impact on morale.

Delegating work to an employee who is not ready to accept the responsibility can have two negative effects:

The job will not get done or not be completed on time.

The failures that result from ineffective delegation will have an understandably bad effect on the affected employee.

When delegating, it is good to always remember that effective delegation of work is not giving up all your authority. The delegate should have a fair amount of freedom, but the manager must retain some control. This will insure that the project is satisfactorily completed.

## 12. Positive Discipline

The word discipline carries with it many negative meanings. It is often used as a synonym for punishment. Yet discipline is also used to refer to the spirit that exists in a successful ball team where team members are willing to consider the needs of the team as more important than their own.

Positive discipline in a business is an atmosphere of mutual trust and common purpose in which all your employees understand the company rules as well as the objectives, and do everything possible to support them.

Any disciplinary program has, as its base, that all of your employees have a clear understanding of exactly what is expected of them. This is why a concise set of rules and standards must exist that is fair, clear, realistic and communicated. Once the standards and rules are known by all employees, discipline can be enforced equitably and fairly.

A good set of rules need not be more than one page, but prove essential to the success of a small business. A few guidelines for establishing a climate of positive discipline are given below:

There must be rules and standards, which are communicated clearly and administered fairly.

Rules and standards must be reasonable.

Rules should be communicated so they are known and understood by all employees. An employee manual can help with communicating rules.

While a rule or a standard is in force, employees are expected to adhere to it.

Even though rules exist, people should know that if a personal problem or a unique situation makes the rule exceptionally harsh, the rule may be modified or an exception be granted.

There should be no favorites and privileges should be granted only when they can also be granted to other employees in similar circumstances. This means that it must be possible to explain to other employees, who request a similar privilege with less justification, why the privilege cannot be extended to them in their particular situation.

Employees must be aware that they can and should voice dissatisfaction with any rules or standards they consider unreasonable as well as with working conditions they feel hazardous, discomforting or burdensome.

Employees should understand the consequences of breaking a rule without permission. Large companies have disciplinary procedures for minor violations which could apply equally well in small companies. They usually call for one or two friendly reminders. If the problem continues, there is a formal, verbal warning, then a written warning, and if the employee persists in violating rules, there would be a suspension and/or dismissal. In violations of more serious rules, fewer steps would be used. It is not easy to communicate this procedure since it should not be so firm that it can be expressed in writing. If it is made clear to employees who violate a rule at the first reminder, the procedure soon becomes understood by all.

There should be an appeals procedure when an employee feels you have made an unfair decision. At the very least, the employee should be aware that you are willing to reconsider your own decision at a later time.

Employees should be consulted when rules are set.

There should be recognition for good performance, reliability and loyalty. Negative comments, when they are necessary, will be accepted as helpful if employees also receive feedback when things go well.

No matter how good the atmosphere of positive discipline in your business, rules are bound to be broken, by some people, from time to time. In those situations, corrective action is sometimes necessary. In some rare cases, the violation may be so severe that serious penalties are necessary. If an employee is caught in the act of stealing or deliberately destroys company property, summary dismissal may be necessary. In all other severe cases, a corrective interview is needed to determine the reasons for the problem and to establish what penalty, if any, is appropriate. Such an interview should include all, or most, of the following steps:

Outlining the problem to the employee, including an explanation of the rule or procedure that was broken.

Allowing the employee to explain his or her side of the story. This step will often bring out problems which need to be resolved to avoid rule violations in the future.

Exploring with the employee what should be done to prevent a recurrence of the problem.

Reaching agreement with the employee on the corrective action that should be taken.

## 13. Dealing with Employee Grievances

When discipline is based heavily on enforcement, complaints will inevitably arise from too rigid adherence to rules or from excessive penalties for violations. But discipline related problems are not the most frequent sources of grievances. Dissatisfactions leading to grievances can come from almost anywhere. Complaints about discrimination and favoritism in work assignments, work standards, or physical working conditions are frequent sources of grievances. It is important to remember, though, that anything about which an employee is dissatisfied can lead to a serious grievance. Grievances need not necessarily be based on real problems; they can be the result of misunderstandings.

If a positive climate exists, in which there is considerable trust between employees and manager, dissatisfaction rarely turns into grievances.

Even in the best environment though, the people who work for you will occasionally feel unhappy about something. They may not get paid on time, or may feel that the room is too hot, too cold, drafty or too dark. They may feel that they deserve a merit increase, or you may have hurt their feelings inadvertently. When this happens; good personnel policies require that employees know how they can express their dissatisfaction and obtain some consideration.

A written grievance procedure, known to employees, can be very helpful in creating a positive atmosphere. It informs employees how they can obtain a hearing on their problems and it assures that you, the owner/manager, become aware that the problem exists. When employees know that someone will listen to them, grievances are less serious and hearing a complaint carefully often is half the job of resolving it.

A good grievance procedure begins with the manager making it a point to be actively looking for signs of possible sources of dissatisfaction, and by noticing changes in employee behavior which signal that a problem may exist. This often makes it possible to handle a situation when it is still easy to resolve. Positive and effective grievance prevention requires, besides the positive discipline steps discussed previously in this section, a few steps which will assure that the best possible solution to the problem is found. Such steps could include:

**1. Discussion, on a one-to-one basis between the employee and you, or if there is a supervisor, with him or her.** Often misunderstandings are cleared up at this point and that ends the grievance. If more than a misunderstanding is involved, a compromise solution can often be found at this point.

There are a number of steps which you, or your supervisor, should follow to assure the best results from such a discussion:

a. Make sure that the employee is comfortable and that your conversation will not be disturbed. An atmosphere of concern and trust is necessary and these precautions can help to start the discussion on a positive note.

b. Listen to the employee attentively and hear him or her out. This will help you more clearly understand the entire problem, not only the immediate cause of the dissatisfaction. There is often more than one thing which disturbs an employee and contributes to the problem.

c. Explain how you see the situation.

d. When all the facts are known, try to come to some mutual understanding or workable compromise. If that is impossible, suggest that you will think about the situation and that the employee should do the same thing. Set a specific date when you will let the employee know what it is that you can, and will do.

e. Follow up on the situation. Make certain that you carry through on all aspects of your decision. If you promised to review something, or to have something fixed, be sure that these really happen. Otherwise employees will not feel that you are sincere with them when you discuss their complaints and dissatisfactions with them.

**2. If disagreement continues, employees should be aware that they can bring the subject up again for further discussion or that they can take it to the owner/manager if their initial discussion was with a supervisor.**

**3. Some small businesses use the managers of neighboring businesses to serve as mediators in such disputes.** If that is done, the business owners agree to help each other in such situations. The "mediator" talks independently to employee and owner and thus brings an impartial point of view to the situation. A competent mediator can make both sides see the situation clearer, and it is therefore more likely that a mutually satisfactory solution can be found.

If a mediator is used, his or her role should be clarified; that function is to explore and seek various possible solutions that might be acceptable to both sides, not to suggest specific solutions.

This guide has presented ways to implement a grievance procedure in a small business. There are several positive results of a good grievance procedure:

1. Providing relief for any negative feelings of employees, before these feelings are released in non-constructive ways - being late, not reporting for work, etc.

2. Restoring employee morale by clearing misunderstandings and improving working conditions.

3. Notifying management of any dissatisfactions at an early stage.

## 14. Communicating With Your Employees

As the manager of a small business you not only have the day-today responsibilities of operating the business, but also the responsibility to establish and administer the disciplinary procedure and to effectively handle grievances and complaints. Your actions are the major factor in determining the human relations climate in your firm. Communication provides the "key" to successfully meeting these responsibilities.

Large corporations recognize this responsibility and use many different media to assure that employees understand, and are kept informed of all matters of interest to them. Small businesses often fail to recognize this need, even though, when compared to large organizations, they have a distinct advantage.

It is certainly much easier to communicate with 5, 10, or 100 employees, than with thousands. Yet, in spite of their advantage, many small companies have poor and inadequate communication with their employees.

Part of the problem lies in recognizing what your employees need to know about the work they're doing, and the company itself, and part of it is that owner/managers often believe that they do keep employees informed. The more employees know, the more they feel part of the company.

There are many things on which employees should receive information, either regularly or when the occasion arises. These include:

vacation plans

holiday plans

benefits

overtime and other special work schedules and

any plans about changes in the work or work environment such as:

new products and services

moves of furniture or work places

etc.                                                                                        .

In addition, it is desirable to keep employees informed about matters affecting the company:

how it is doing, and where it is going

improvements in company operation

laws or regulations affecting company operations

new contracts

new product plans

Employees want to know most everything about their company, and more importantly, matters affecting them; keeping them informed, therefore, satisfies an important need.

There are two channels of communications through which employees obtain information:

The informal communications network which includes any

conversations you have with individual employees or small groups of employees. The informal network also includes the rumors which spring up when there is concern about something but no direct information.

The formal communications network includes such methods or procedures as:

**a. Any regular meetings you (or your supervisors) may hold with employees** to brief them on matters of interest and to discuss anything of concern to the company or to them, including problems with production, standards or rules, as well as any concerns they may have. Such meetings provide considerable feelings of belonging to employees and bring many suggestions on how specific projects, as well as overall operations can be improved.

**b. A small employee manual**, which proves useful in the orientation of a new employee to your company, but also serves as a reference on policy benefits, important rules, safety programs and procedures for handling grievances.

**c. An organized bulletin board with current information.** Notices of holidays, changes of shift or work schedules, new policies, emergency telephone numbers and any other information that would prove of interest to employees, can be posted on such a bulletin board. Notice of personal information regarding your employees - congratulations on birthdays, births, marriages - can also be posted.

**d. Posters promoting safety, health, and good housekeeping procedures** can also add to a good communication climate as long as they are kept clean and neat, and changed regularly.

## 15. Managing Employee Benefits

Employee benefits play an important role in the lives of employees and their families and have a significant financial impact on any business, large or small. Most businesses operate in an environment where an educated work force has come to expect a comprehensive benefit program. The absence of such a program or the installation of an inadequate program can seriously hinder your ability to attract and retain good personnel. Further, benefits can be costly as well as administratively burdensome. It is important that you, as an employer, are aware of the relevant issues and that you are prepared to make an informed decision on selecting a benefit program.

### What Makes Up a Comprehensive Employee Benefit Program?

While a complete explanation of the numerous employee benefit plans is beyond the scope of this guide, it is important that you attain a basic understanding of the type of plans available. For purposes of this guide, an employee benefit program can be broken down into four components: legally required benefits, health and welfare benefits, retirement benefits and prerequisites.

Legally required benefit plans are mandated by law and the systems necessary to administer such plans are well established. These plans include social security, workers' compensation and unemployment compensation.

Health and welfare benefits and retirement benefits can be viewed as benefits provided to work in conjunction with statutory benefits to protect employees from financial hazards such as:

illness,

disability,

death, and

retirement (cessation of employment)

Health and welfare plans are perhaps the most visible of all the benefit program components. These benefits include:

medical care,

dental care,

vision care,

short-term disability,

long-term disability,

life insurance,

accidental death and dismemberment insurance,

dependent care, and legal assistance

Since health and welfare benefit plans provide the more visible and tangible benefits, they play a key part in the reception of a benefit program.

Retirement plans are instituted to help ensure that employees are able to maintain their accustomed standard of living upon retirement. Retirement benefit plans basically fall into two categories: 1) defined contribution plans which provide employees with an account balance at retirement, and 2) defined benefit plans which provide employees with a predetermined amount of income at retirement. Each of these categories includes various kinds of plans but only the most popular plans will be addressed.

Prerequisites encompass any additional benefits an employer promises, which may include automobiles, country club memberships or out-of-town conventions.

## Selecting An Employee Benefit Program

Designing and implementing an employee benefit program is a complicated process that should be planned with the aid of a benefit professional. Employee benefit professionals are generally available in consulting firms, insurance companies, law firms or accounting firms. An employee benefit program should be designed to meet the individual needs of your company. Therefore, before consulting a professional, you should consider the following:

What should the program accomplish in the long run? In other words, what are the objectives of the program?

What is the maximum amount you can afford to spend on a program?

What is your administrative capability?

Understand your employee group today and what it may look like in the future - what kind of program would fit your employee population?

Do you want employee input? In which benefits are employees interested?

When you have completed items 2 through 5, you may need to reevaluate item 1 to determine the feasibility of your objectives.

It is important to consider each item listed above when selecting a benefit program. You will be very well equipped to consult a professional if you have carefully examined each item. You should choose your consultant carefully to ensure that you retain one who will take the time to understand your business requirements and your short- and long-term financial capability.

## Which Plan Is Right For Your Company?

In general, it should be noted that certain plans will be more suitable than others based on an employer's financial situation and the demographics of the employee group. Employers who are not confident of their future income may not want to start a defined benefit plan which will require a specific level of contributions. However, if the employees are fairly young, a profit sharing plan can result in a more significant and more appreciated benefit than a defined benefit plan. If your work force is composed mainly of older employees, a defined benefit plan will be more beneficial to them but more expensive to maintain.

## Prerequisite Benefit Plans

Many key employees have come to expect certain additional benefits from their employers. here is

a list of various types of prerequisite benefits. It is your option as an employer to choose among this wide variety of benefits:

Company automobile

Extra vacation

Special parking privileges

Personal expense accounts

Spouse traveling on company business

Sabbaticals (with pay)

Professional membership

Loans/mortgages

Club memberships

Chauffeur

Estate planning

Financial counseling

Medical expense

reimbursement

Travel clubs

Credit cards

Home entertainment

allowance

Physical examination

Executive dining room

## Communications

Effective employee communications are essential to successfully introduce or maintain an employee benefit program. Too often employees do not understand or are not aware of the various components of their benefit program. Your benefit program will not achieve its long-term objectives if it is not effectively communicated. Good communications will ensure that you gain the full benefit of your program. Further, there are legally required communications which must be provided to employees in retirement plans and health and welfare plans.

## Conclusion

Hopefully, the information provided in this publication will be useful to you in selecting, implementing and maintaining an effective employee benefit program. Benefits play too significant a role in the success of a business to allow decisions to be made in an uninformed manner. Generally, the point of an employee benefit program is to provide employees with protection when they need it. An effective benefit program should shield your employees from the financial burden of illness, disability, retirement or death. Small business managers who demonstrate a sense of caring for their employees by providing well-balanced benefit program will take a major step in developing a stable and productive work force.

## 16. Developing a Training Program (Checklist)

This guide is designed to help owner-managers of small firms set up a systematic program for training their employees. The questions are designed to provide a step-by-step approach to the task of organizing and conducting a successful program of employee training.

Whether you are considering a continuous program or a one-shot course, the questions should stimulate your thinking. Many of them involve alternatives which you need to resolve in setting up the program.

Use this checklist as a guide. The experience of other companies in training can provide additional guides. However, in thinking about a training program for your company, consider each question and mark it "yes" or "no" in light of the training needs of your particular situation.

### What is the Goal of the Training?

The questions in this section are designed to help the owner-manager define the objective or goal to be achieved by a training program. Whether the objective is to conduct initial training, to provide for upgrading employees, or to retrain for changing job assignments, the goal should be spelled out before developing the plan for the training program.

1. Do you want to improve the performance of your employees?

2. Will you improve your employees by training them to perform their present tasks better?

3. Do you need to prepare employees for newly developed or modified jobs?

4. Is training needed to prepare employees for promotion?

5. Is the goal to reduce accidents and increase safety practices?

6 Should the goal be to improve employee attitudes especially about waste and spoilage practices?

7. Do you need to improve the handling of materials in order to break production bottlenecks?

8. Is the goal to orient new employees to their jobs?

9. Will you need to teach new employees about over-all operation?

10. Do you need to train employees so they can help teach new workers in an expansion program?

## What Does the Employee Need to Learn?

Once the objective or goal of the program is set, you will need to determine the subject matter. The following questions are designed to help you decide what the employee needs in terms of duties, responsibilities, and attitudes.

11. Can the job be broken down into steps for training purposes?

12. Are there standards of quality which trainees can be taught?

13. Are there certain skills and techniques which trainees must learn?

14. Are there hazards and safety practices which must be taught?

15. Have you established the methods which employees must use to avoid or minimize waste and spoilage?

16. Are there materials handling techniques that must be taught?

17. Have you determined the best way for the trainees to operate the equipment?

18. Are there performance standards which employees must meet?

19. Are there attitudes that need improvement or modifications?

20. Will information on your products help employees to do a better job?

21. Should the training include information about the location and use of tool cribs and so on?

22. Will the employee need instruction about departments other than his or her own?

## What Type of Training?

The type of training to be offered has an important bearing on the balance of the program. Some types lend themselves to achieving all of the objectives or goals, while others are limited. Therefore you should review the advantages of each type in relation to your objective or goal.

23. Can you train on-the-job so that employees can produce while they learn?

24. Should you have classroom training conducted by a paid instructor?

25. Will a combination of scheduled on-the-job training and vocational classroom instruction work best for you.

26. Can your goal be achieved with a combination of on-the-job training and correspondence courses?

## What Method of Instruction?

One or more methods of instruction may be used. Some are better for one type of training than another: for example, lectures are good for imparting knowledge, and demonstrations are good for teaching skills.

27. Does the subject matter call for a lecture or series of lectures?

28. Should the instructor follow up with discussion sessions?

29. Does the subject matter lend itself to demonstrations?

30. Can operating problems be simulated in a classroom?

31. Can the instructor direct trainees while they perform the job?

## What Audio-Visual Aids Will You Use?

Audio-visual aids help the instructor to make points and enable the trainees to grasp and retain the instructions.

32. Will a manual of interaction - including job instruction sheets - be used?

33. Will trainees be given an outline of the training program?

34. Can outside textbooks and other printed materials be used?

35. If the training lends itself to the use of video, film strips or slides, can you get ones that show the basic operation?

36. Have you drawings or photographs of the machinery, equipment or products which could be enlarged and used?

37. Do you have miniatures or models of machinery and equipment which can be used to demonstrate the operation?

## What Physical Facilities Will You Need?

The type of training, the method of instruction and the audio-visuals will determine the physical facilities needed for the training.

In turn, the necessary physical facilities will determine the location of the training. For example, if a certain production machine is necessary, the training would be conducted in the shop.

38. If the training cannot be conducted on the production floor, do you have a conference room or a lunch room in which it can be conducted?

39. Should the training be conducted off the premises, as in a nearby school restaurant, hotel or motel?

40. Will the instructor have the necessary tools, such as a blackboard, lectern, film projector and a microphone if needed).

41. Will there be sufficient seating and writing surfaces (if needed) for trainee?

42. If equipment is to be used, will each trainee be provided with his or her own?

## What About the Timing?

The length of the training program will vary according to the needs of your company, the material to be learned, the ability of the instructor, and the ability of the trainees to learn.

43. Should the training be conducted part-time and during working hours?

44. Should the sessions be held after working hours?

45. Will the instruction cover a predetermined period of time? (For example, 4 weeks, 6 weeks, 3 months.)

46. Can the length of each session and the number of sessions per week be established?

## Who Will Be Selected As Instructor?

The success of training depends to a great extent on the instructor. A qualified one could achieve good results even with limited resources. On the other hand, an untrained instructor may be unsuccessful even with the best program. You may want to use more than one person as instructor.

47. Can you fill in as an instructor?

48. Do you have a personnel manager who has the time and the ability to do the instructing?

49. Can your supervisor or department heads handle the instructions?

50. Should a skilled employee be used as the instructor?

51. Will you have to train the instructor?

52. Is there a qualified outside instructor available for employment on a part-time basis?

## Who Should Be Selected?

Employees should be selected for training on the basis of goal of the program as well as their aptitudes, physical capabilities, previous experiences, and attitudes.

53. Should new employees be hired for training?

54. Should the training of new employees be a condition of employment?

55. Would you prefer trainees with previous experience in the work?

56. Are there present employees who need training?

57. Will you consider employees presently in lower rated jobs who have the aptitude to learn?

58. Is the training to be a condition for promotion?

59. Will the training be made available to handicapped employees whose injury occurred while employed by the company?

60. Should employees displaced by job changes, departmental shutdowns, automation, and so on be given the opportunity to be trained in other jobs?

## What Will the Program Cost

It may be desirable to compute the costs of your training before starting the program. Thus, you can budget sufficient funds for the program and use the budget as a tool for keeping training costs in line.

62. Should you change the program for the space, the machines, and materials used?

63. Will the wages of trainees be included?

64. If the instructor is an employee, will his or her pay be included in the costs?

65. Will the time you and others spend in preparing and administrating the program be part of the costs?

66. If usable production results from the sessions, should the results of it be deducted from costs of the program?

## What Checks or Controls Will You Use?

The results of the training program need to be checked to determine the extent to which the original goal or objective was achieved.

67. Can you check the results of the training against the goal or objective?

68. Can standards of learning time be established against which to check the progress of the trainees?

69. Can data on trainee performance be developed before, during, and after training?

70. Will records be kept on the progress of each trainee?

71. Will trainees be tested on the knowledge and skills acquired?

72. Will the instructor rate each trainee during and at the end of the course?

73. Will the training be followed up periodically by a supervisor or department head to determine the long-range effects of the training?

74. Should you personally check and control the program?

## How Should the Program Be Publicized?

Publicizing the company's training program in the community helps attract qualified job applicants. Publicity inside the company helps motivate employees to improve themselves.

75. If the program is announced to employees, will the announcement be made before the program starts? During the program?

76. Are pictures to be taken of the training sessions and used on bulletin boards and in local newspapers?

77. Should employees who complete the training be awarded certificates?

78. Should the certificates be presented at a special affair, such as a dinner?

79. When the certificates are awarded, will you invite the family of the trainees?

80. Should the local newspaper, radio, and TV people be invited to the "graduation" exercises?

## 17. Using Temporary Help Services

How do you cope with unexpected personnel shortages? Many businesses are facing this question whether the cause is seasonal peaking, inventory taking, special projects, several employees on sick leave at the same time, or an unexpected increase in business.

Many companies are finding a convenient and economical solution to such problems in the services of temporary personnel firms. This guide explains these services, points out some of their advantages and outlines some steps that can be taken to ensure getting the best possible results from using them.

Almost every business needs extra help at one time or another. A rush order comes in. The work load suddenly zooms and then drops back to normal when the rush order is finished. More employees than usual are absent because of illness or vacations. A special project has to have attention right away. Seasonal demands must be met or inventories must be taken without disrupting your usual business. The extra-heavy workload puts a strain on you, on your employees, and on your budget because of the overtime it requires.

These temporary shortages of personnel are especially hard for the owner-manager of the smaller businesses to handle. Their staff is small. There is little leeway for shifting schedules. Yet they cannot afford to keep on their payrolls workers who are not needed when the workload is at a normal level.

The use of temporary personnel is a relatively new approach to solving many of the personnel problems facing both large and small businesses. You can hire these extra workers by recruiting them yourself or using a private employment agency. Or you can call on a temporary personnel service firm to meet your needs. These specialized firms are usually equipped to supply you with a wide variety of people, or, in the case of some of the larger services, handle a complete department including supervisors and workers.

## What Is a Temporary Personnel Service?

A temporary personnel service is not an employment agency. Like many service firms, it hires people as its own employees and assigns them to companies requesting assistance. This means that when you use such a service, you are not hiring an employee; you are buying the use of their time. The temporary personnel firm is responsible for payroll, bookkeeping, tax deductions, workers compensation, fringe benefits and all other similar costs connected with the employee. You are relieved of the burden of recruiting, interviewing, screening and even testing and training if these are necessary. Most national temporary personnel companies also offer performance guarantees and fidelity bonding at no added cost to their clients. In addition, you are relieved of the need for government forms and for reporting withholding tax, etc. The temporary service firm takes these responsibilities.

You may contract for a secretary, a word processing operator, a bookkeeper, a switchboard operator, a product demonstrator, a packer, added sales personnel or any of many other types of office, professional, and industrial workers. You may contract for temporary personnel for a day or for a much longer period of time.

Whatever help you need, a temporary personnel service will try to provide the right person for the job. Some temporary personnel companies specialize in one type of help, such as office workers. Others can supply a broad range of personnel from unskilled labor to accountants and engineers.

Some of the other areas where temporary personnel are profitable to use include a temporary second shift to allow you to make the most use of expensive equipment investments. Sales blitzes to introduce new products, special quarterly or year end invoicing problems, special telephone sales programs or order taking, and seasonal catalog sales are examples. Some companies contract for teams of temporary people to perform microfilming of documents, retrieval of information, and maintenance of files. Temporaries also find wide use at trade shows, product sampling or demonstrations. National temporary firms can offer the smaller company a means of handling a national marketing effort that allows them to compete with larger organizations without excessive permanent overhead.

## Why Not Hire Your Own Temporary Personnel?

Hiring temporary workers on your own has several important disadvantages. For one thing, it may hamper your efforts to attract good permanent employees. Layoffs when an emergency has passed can lower moral among the regular employees and, if it happens too often, gives your firm a reputation for instability.

Another disadvantage is that you may not be able to get help when you need it. There may be times when the labor market is tight and the skills you need are not readily available. Also, you may feel that the time you spend in orienting new people for short-term employment is largely wasted.

The financial aspects of hiring short-term personnel is also of major importance. On the surface it may appear that using temporary personnel costs more than hiring additional employees yourself, but there are many costs that are not usually considered. As an example, mandatory costs, such as social security, unemployment insurance, workers compensation, etc., amounts to over 11% of the basic salary. Payment for time not worked including vacations, holidays and sick days, amounts to almost 9%. Then there are company paid benefits such as health insurance, pension plans, discounts and recordkeeping, payroll and other paperwork amounts to another 6-7%. Total hidden costs are in the neighborhood of 42%.

## Advantages of Using a Temporary Services Firm

People supplied by a temporary service firm are quickly available. Usually they can start the day after the request has been made and, in some cases, can even be made available the same day. Experienced and well qualified, they need little, if any, assistance. They usually walk in and begin functioning right away. Using people from this source, you can adjust to fast-breaking opportunities or problems without interrupting your regular production schedule.

Some companies need temporary help every week for a few hours, for example for payroll computation. Others need temporary workers for full days at various time - regularly or occasionally.

The hourly rate you pay a temporary service firm is generally higher than the base hourly or weekly salary you would pay an employee you hired yourself; however, the cost of getting the work done is less. Using a temporary services firm does away with many personnel and recordkeeping operations that are costly and time consuming. The costs of maintaining records and filing forms for fringe benefits, payroll taxes and administration are eliminated. So are the costs of advertising, screening responses, interviewing, testing, checking references and all of the other functions needed to bring a new employee into the company. In addition, you save the cost of training, of overtime and idle periods. When you use a temporary firm you pay for the actual time worked only. You do not have to pay for lunch hours, vacations, sick days and other areas of non-productivity. Every company has some department where turnover is high. By using temporary personnel for such jobs you can improve your turnover statistics .

## When Not to Use a Temporary Service

In considering whether or not to use a temporary service, the disadvantages to your company as well as the advantages must be considered. In some cases regular employees who lose overtime pay because of the temporary workers will become a morale problem. In other cases the work may be highly specialized and require a period of training, even though it may be short. This may make the use of temporary personnel less economical.

Basically, if you need temporary personnel for a period of six months or more it is advisable to hire a full time employee. There are also cases where the job may be so complex that it requires a great deal of supervision for a worker who is unfamiliar with your way of doing things. In such instances, it may be more economical to pay overtime to a regular employee than to use a temporary worker.

## What Will It Cost?

Charges by temporary service firms vary widely with the type of help you are contracting for. Obviously, rates will be higher for the more skilled office or industrial worker than they will be for the less skilled. Rates vary from city to city also since most temporary service firms pay their employees the going rate in that particular area for a given job. They charge you in accordance with this rate plus a basic markup that covers administrative costs plus a fair profit for the service.

You pay an hourly rate to the temporary service firm. They, in turn, pay the employee for the hours worked and take care of payroll taxes, workmen's compensation and so on.

Most reputable services do not charge you for the hours worked by an unsatisfactory worker if you let them know promptly that you are dissatisfied. Generally, you must notify them within four hours after the employee reports for work, but this provision varies with individual firms.

What you save by using temporary services depends on your individual situation. If you are to get the most for your investment, you must carefully analyze your needs and plan carefully to make the best possible use of the time and skills of the employee being supplied by the temporary service firm. The guidelines that follow will be helpful.

## How to Select a Temporary Service Firm?

There are a great many temporary service firms throughout the country. Many are located in large population centers, some operating regionally and a few nationally. If you are likely to need temporary workers, it is a good idea to do some exploring in advance.

Check with you local Chamber of Commerce, your attorney, your accountant, your banker. Look in the yellow pages of the telephone directory under "Employment, Temporary" or "Employment Contractors - Temporary Help" or a similar heading.

Try to meet in person with the executive of the firm you select. A short discussion will help them understand your operation, problems and needs. You, in turn, can gain an understanding of just what service the company provides.

You should evaluate the company and its ability to serve you properly by most of these factors.

**Reliability:** Is the service a well established company with a history of success and financial stability? You might want to check their annual report if its a public company or ask for a certified financial statement to determine if they are a stable organization.

**Recruiting:** Competition for skilled, reliable employees in today's labor market is intense. The firm that has an aggressive recruiting program is more likely to have the most skilled and reliable employees to send you.

**Testing and evaluating:** What method of testing and evaluating personnel is used to assure that you will receive quality people when needed? Does the firm check references?

**Training Programs:** Certain skills are always in short supply regardless of employment conditions. Does the company train people in various aspects of office work, such as modern office equipment, word processing equipment, records management, upgrading of typing and shorthand skills, etc.? The company should carefully train operators on the newest types of equipment and in the newest techniques.

**Retention Programs:** Does the company have a good program to keep qualified employees for longer periods of time? This can assure you that you will again get qualified people when you need them in the near future.

**Professional Permanent Staff:** If you want to deal with knowledgeable professionals who will know and understand your needs, the temporary service firm should be staffed by people experienced in the personnel field.

**Knowledge of Your Needs:** Does the firm make any effort to investigate your needs and do they seem to understand what you are discussing with them as far as needs for personnel?

**Prompt Service:** The temporary service firm that has a supply of people available for you on short notice can be most important when you are in a rush.

**Quality Control:** Does the company make some effort to check back with you and determine the quality of the individual as far as they relate to your work?

**Insurance Protection:** Does the firm protect your company with ample insurance coverage including fidelity bonds, workers compensation, and other problems that might arise?

**Guarantee:** Does the temporary service firm guarantee your satisfaction with each and every temporary employee sent to you? Does it have a refund or guarantee policy? What are its terms?

## Plan Early

The key to the successful use of temporary employees is in planning what type of help you will need, how much and when. The amount of accurate information you give to the temporary service firm will determine the efficiency they will have in supplying the correct people for your needs.

To plan properly for the use of a temporary service you must answer these questions:

How seasonal is my business?

Do any of my regular employees have to work overtime to meet peak workloads? If so, what does the overtime cost?

If any extensive amount of overtime is needed, will there be a performance lag and possible morale problems during regular working hours?

With better planning could I spread out any of the peak work loads through the year?

Are my deliveries made on schedule?

Do customers often come up with rush jobs?

If so, can I get them to plan their needs further in advance?

Are my employees' vacations scheduled not to interfere with peak seasons?

What extra help do I need to cope with these problems and reduce costs?

Plan discussion sessions with key personnel, those involved with planning day to day operations. Study your production schedule. Note peak periods. Compare this year with previous years. A pattern will begin to emerge and you will be able to see where some extra help would have avoided problems and kept your costs down. Many temporary service firms will supply trained personnel to advise you in this regard.

## What to Do When the Time Comes

If it is decided that you can use temporary help, it is extremely important that you inform them of exactly what is needed. A good temporary firm will have detailed description forms about your company and the positions you are filling with their services so that they can furnish the proper employee for you. They will ask for information such as the department they will be working in, the duration of the assignment, your working hours, your dress code, smoking rules, and other information that is important for the service to know. Will you be needing a copy typist or a clerk-typist for example? Does the secretarial position require shorthand or are there machine transcriptions to do? What type of software and office equipment are involved? Are there any special knowledges or skills needed? You will find that by informing the service of your exact needs you will have qualified people furnished to you and will not be paying for skills that are not needed for your individual assignment. Most of the larger temporary service firms have special advisors who will work with you and help you plan ahead. In summary:

## Estimate your needs

Decide what the specific requirements of the job are. Exactly what talents do you need? How long will you need the employee?

Don't ask for someone with higher qualifications than the work calls for or the cost will be unnecessarily high. On the other hand, don't try to economize by getting under-qualified help and then expecting the worker to carry out tasks that he or she isn't prepared to handle.

## Give the temporary-help service full information

If the temporary personnel firm is to help you get the best results at the lowest possible cost, you must give its people detailed information about the work to be done. Tell them the nature of your business, the working hours, when and how long you'll need help, the skills required, the types of equipment to be operated. You may want to send samples of the work to be done, if it is feasible. Be sure to give the exact location of your business, transportation available, parking information, and the name and title of the person to whom the temporary employee is to report.

## Preparing for the Temporary Employee

A few steps taken before the temporary employee reports for work will do much to make the association a success, both for the employee and for you.

## ONE - Arrange for supervision

Appoint one of your permanent employees to supervise the temporary employee and check on the progress of the work from time to time. Be sure this supervisor understands the job to be done and just what his or her own responsibility is.

## TWO - Tell your permanent employees

It's a good idea to let your staff know that you are taking on extra help and that it will be temporary. Explain why the extra help is needed and ask them to cooperate with the new employee in any way possible.

## THREE - Prepare the physical facilities

Have everything ready before the temporary worker arrives. The work to be done should be organized and laid out so that the employee can begin producing with a minimum of time spent in adjusting to the job and the surrounding. See that the materials needed are available and the equipment is in place and in good working order.

## FOUR - Plan the work load

Don't set up schedules that are impossible to complete within the time you allot. Try to stay within the time limits you gave the temporary-help service, but plan to extend the time period, if necessary, rather than crowd the employee. Rushing and overwork can result in costly mistakes.

## FIVE - Prepare detailed instructions

Describe your type of business, the products you manufacture or the services you offer. Be specific in outlining the procedures your company follows. Most employees of temporary-help services adjust quickly to the methods of an individual firm because of their varied experience.

## The Work Begins

You've made all the preparations. The employee has arrived and is ready to start work. What now? How do you get a temporary worker started? What should you expect? What if you're not satisfied?

This is the crucial stage of the relation between your company and the temporary employee. Get off to a good start and the rest will go smoothly.

## ONE - Help the employee settle in

Receive the temporary employee as you would receive one hired on a permanent basis. Make the person feel like a member of your team. Explain where to hang coats, the location of the washroom, the lunch hour, coffee breaks, and so on.

Introduce the temporary employee to the permanent employee who will supervise the work.

Introduce the temporary employee also to permanent employees in the same department. Explain that "Ms. Jones will be here for a few days to help out". Or, "Mr. Smith will be here this week to help get out the rush job."

## TWO - Explain the job

Go over the work assignment and the instructions. Explain company routines. Make your directions as simple as possible and provide samples of the work to be done. If the work is complex, explain it clearly and make certain that your explanation is understood. Assure the temporary employee of your staff's cooperation and willingness to help, and show your own interest and concern.

## THREE - Don't expect the impossible

How much can you expect from a temporary employee? Fully as much as you contracted for with the service firm. Most employees of temporary personnel firms perform well. They are experienced and versatile. Because they have worked for a variety of businesses, they have learned to adapt quickly to a new situation, and they know that future assignments depend on their doing satisfactory work.

But don't expect the impossible. Don't overload temporary employees - make a slight allowance for the fact that they are not familiar with your business and its operations. Check the work occasionally, ask for any questions, never leave the employee feeling stranded or left out. At the same time, don't make them nervous by hovering over them. And don't push or prod too much.

## Judging the Overall Results

Within a few hours after the temporary worker has reported, you will be able to judge how the work is going. If you are not satisfied, you should not hesitate to call the temporary service firm and inform them of the problems. Most reliable temporary service firms will call you to see how the person is working out and take corrective action if required.

A good temporary service firm will ask you to evaluate the employee's work at the end of the assignment.

You have a right to expect a conscientious, interested employee who will put in a full day's work.

You should also judge the use of temporary services in your business operation. To do this, you should keep these points in mind to help you plan for future needs:

Did the productivity of the employee justify the cost? Was the work completed accurately and effectively?

Did it benefit the impact on your overall operations? Were there any disadvantages?

After you have evaluated the above points, you can consult with your key people and the temporary service firm to evaluate your needs for the future. You may be able to work out a program for hiring temporary personnel throughout the year so that you will be fully covered for work loads at all times.